M000295290

"Few characteristics mean mor
To be resilient, a person must h
show love and persistence. This
that are essential to the well being of children and youth and the
people blessed to serve and live with them."

— **Stevan J. Kukic, Ph.D.**
Vice President,
Sopris West Educational Services

"We are fortunate to have innovative educators like Edward P.
Fiszer, Ed.D. in our school systems! In *Daily Positives: Inspiring
Greatness in the Next Generation,* Dr. Fiszer shares messages of
hope, inspiration, and "how to" with all of us. What better gift for
every teacher and parent you know?"

— **Jo Condrill, M.S. author, consultant, and seminar leader**
Take Charge of Your Life: Dare to Pursue Your Dreams

"Daily Positives:Inspiring Greatness in the Next Generation
provides a wide-range of positive messages that help teachers and
parents encourage children towards optimism in their daily life.
Many of these major thinkers give wonderful ways to look at the
world and to negate messages sent out by the mass media."

— **Joyce H. Burstein, Ed.D.**
Assistant Professor
Department of Elementary Education
California State University, Northridge

"Daily Positives:Inspiring Greatness in the Next Generation is a
great resource for a new or veteran principal to have at her/his
fingertips. As I was preparing my carefully selected words to
inspire the new freshmen students coming to our campus, I
turned to Dr. Fiszer's book for themes and words of inspiration. This great book allows students to reflect on the wisdom
of others."

— **Gloria M. Martinez, Ed.D.**
Academic Principal
Palisades Charter High School

Daily

Positives

Inspiring Greatness
in the
Next Generation

Second Edition

Edward P. Fiszer Ed.D.

GoalMinds, Inc.
San Antonio, Texas

Daily Positives: Inspiring Greatness in the Next Generation
Copyright © 2005, 2006 by Edward P. Fiszer, Ed.D.

Published by:
GoalMinds, Inc.
P.O. Box 100903
San Antonio, Texas 78201-8903

All rights reserved. No part of this book may be reproduced or transmitted in any form or by any means, electronic or mechanical, including photocopying, recording, retrieval system, without written permission from the author, except for the inclusion of brief quotations in a review. If you have received this book without a cover, then this version has been counterfeited or you have an unauthorized version.

This text should be used only as a general guide and not as the ultimate source of information. Neither the author nor the publisher make any claims of ownership regarding the quotes/sayings. The quotes used in this edition were used to illustrate the author's point of view.

Please email info@fiszerconcepts.com regarding the source of the quotes or to request permission to make copies.

Printed in the United States of America
Library of Congress Control Number: 2005925083

Publisher's Cataloging-in-Publication
(*Provided by Quality Books, Inc.*)

Fiszer, Edward P. (Edward Peter), 1970-
Daily positives : inspiring greatness in the next
generation / Edward P. Fiszer. -- 2nd ed.
p. cm.
Includes index.
LCCN 2005925083
ISBN-13: 978-0-9740970-1-5
ISBN-10: 0-9740970-1-2
1. Success--Quotations, maxims, etc. I. Title.
BJ1611.2.F559 2006 158.1
QBI06-200090

Contents

About the Author

 Edward P. Fiszer, Ed.D., is the founding principal of NEW Academy Canoga Park, an elementary charter school which emphasizes art and science. He also teaches graduate level courses in education at National University and California State University, Northridge. His extensive background in education has given him a keen familiarity with the power of written and spoken motivational messages. After incorporating inspirational messages into his school's daily announcements, Dr. Fiszer has found that brief, key thoughts can encapsulate the deepest yearnings of the heart as well as the highest aspirations of students and adults alike.

Born and raised in Los Angeles, California, Dr. Fiszer received his Bachelors of Arts degree in history at UCLA and multiple-subject teaching credential at California State University, Northridge. While serving as an elementary school teacher and English language development specialist in Burbank, he attended the Educational Leadership Academy at Pepperdine University for a Master of Science degree in education administration. He returned to UCLA for a doctorate through the Educational Leadership Program, while working as a site administrator in Palmdale.

Dr. Fiszer also coaches and consults on teacher learning, leadership, character development, and special education issues. His presentations are geared toward people who impact children's lives, such as counselors, daycare professionals, parents, grandparents, adoptive parents, school psychologists, medical professionals, and educators. He is a member of the Association for Supervision and Curriculum Development, the Association of California School Administrators, Carskadon Associates, the National Association of Elementary School Principals, and Phi Delta Kappa.

Dr. Fiszer has also completed mediation training through the Los Angeles County Bar Association. A form of conflict resolution, mediation allows the parties involved to clarify the reasons behind the dispute and mutually shape a resolution. Dr. Fiszer uses this training in mediation to help a variety of clients, such as students and educators, divorce and custody situations, and organizations.

Dr. Fiszer's previous publications include How Teachers Learn Best: An Ongoing Professional Development Model, which is an adaptation of his doctoral study and explores the benefits of site-based ongoing professional development versus half-day sessions. Also, Thoughts to Inspire: Daily Messages for Young People is a collection of inspirational quotes and passages created during Dr. Fiszer's years at Pinetree Community School.

On his website, www.fiszerconcepts.com, Dr. Fiszer also offers resume consulting services. He helps his clients create resumes, prepare for interviews, and use the internet to broaden their career search. In his spare time, Dr. Fiszer also enjoys running, tennis, music, film, reading, and writing.

Contact Dr. Fiszer at efiszer@fiszerconcepts.com

This book is dedicated to all those who dare to do what is right while knowingly or unknowingly serving as positive role models for others.

Acknowledgements

Thanks to Jo Condrill, whose experience, wisdom, and generosity have led me to publish.

I am grateful to the students and staff of Pinetree Community School for their positive feedback on the morning announcements.

In addition, I acknowledge and appreciate all those who provided endorsements for my book. Thank you for providing your time, energy, and acknowledgements.

Introduction

The space between thought and action is filled with choice. Regardless of whether the person makes the choice in a matter of seconds or over a long period of time, this space has the potential to make a great impact on the world. This impact may be positive or negative, depending on the person's inspiration.

Inspiration to do the right thing, if consistent, can prime young minds for making positive choices. They can learn the importance of aligning actions with goals, and know that doing good things can make positive changes every day.

Positive reinforcement is the key to keeping an individual's thoughts focused on positive outcomes. Authors Steven Covey, Earl Nightingale, and others encourage the review of goals every morning and every evening. Through customary encouragement in the pursuit of goals, the brain seeks to create equilibrium between the images in a person's mind and reality. For young people, the mind is more likely to link actions to goals if they are consistently reminded what amazing dreams are achievable – particularly through the wisdom of those who have achieved what most consider impossible.

Parents, counselors, teachers, administrators, and mentors can inspire positive actions each day through guidance and meaningful discussions with their students. My elementary students in Southern California hear passages like these read through the school's sound system every morning. These passages can be adapted for any school-age audience, and used as part of a positive start to each day.

Just as a forest ultimately begins with one seed, a single conversation can positively impact an individual's actions and unleash a torrent of positivism on society.

Daily Positives

Take Responsibility For Your Own Improvement
Gilbert Arland

An archer uses a bow and arrow, aims at a target, and tries to shoot the arrow at the very center, or the bulls-eye. Gilbert Arland once said, "When an archer misses the mark, he turns and looks for the fault within himself. Failure to hit the bulls-eye is never the fault of the target or the bow. To improve your aim, improve yourself."

Archers don't blame anyone else for missing the center of the target. The archer thinks about his or her technique and how much more practice may be needed. In the end, only the archer can be responsible for his or her level of improvement.

You can also make greater improvements toward your goals by taking responsibility for your own weaknesses and working through those areas. If you want to be a better athlete, or a better reader, or a better friend, identify the barriers to your success. Focus on areas where you'd like to improve and, if you put in the effort and practice, your skills will improve over time.

Persistence

Mary Kay Ash

Mary Kay Ash once said, "One of the secrets of success is to refuse to let temporary setbacks defeat us."

The most successful people in history, the ones you remember and honor today, are those who didn't let anything stop them. They are the presidents, the inventors, and the pioneers. While Henry Ford was developing automobiles, people told him he was wasting his time. In fact, he failed and ran out of money for his projects five times before he was successful. But he kept going, and now look at how many cars are on the roads.

Pablo Casals, who was a cellist, was once asked why he continued practicing the cello six hours each day. He said, "Because I think I'm making progress." He eventually became the greatest cellist who ever lived.

Dr. Seuss's first children's book was rejected by twenty-seven publishers before it was published. The twenty-eighth publisher sold six million copies of *And to Think That I Saw It on Mulberry Street*. And Dr. Seuss went on to publish many more titles through the years.

No matter how discouraged you become, never let a failure or a problem stop you. Keep going. You will only succeed if you refuse to give up. Figure out what you want to do and keep up the effort until you succeed.

Making and Keeping Friends
Elbert Hubbard

E lbert Hubbard, who was a well-sought-after lecturer and newspaper writer in the early 1900s, wrote, "In order to have friends, you must first be one."

The best friends in the world are the people who sincerely care about others and do nice things without expecting anything in return. They listen and understand. They are supportive and positive. Friends are people who can be trusted. People attract friends when they are honest and do nice things for others. Those who are dishonest and don't do nice things for others have difficulty making and keeping friends.

Today, as you interact with your classmates and teachers, remember the importance of being a friend to others without expecting anything in return. Other people will notice and want to do nice things for you as well.

You Lose By Not Trying

Francis Bacon

Francis Bacon lived from 1561 through 1626. He was an author and philosopher who believed in trying as hard as possible to solve problems and overcome challenges.

He wrote, "There is no comparison between that which is lost by not succeeding and that which is lost by not trying."

In other words, people who always try new things have a better chance at being truly successful, even though they may not be successful the first time. But people who avoid new things rob themselves of new experiences and new joys that come from meeting challenges.

Today, increase your chances of being successful by seeking new challenges and trying new activities. Don't back down at the first sign of failure. Keep working to overcome your challenges.

Express Yourself Through Your Choices
Eleanor Roosevelt

E leanor Roosevelt was a great woman who made a positive impact on the world through the choices she made. She was married to President Franklin D. Roosevelt, and was known as the "First Lady of the World" for her world-wide human rights efforts. She helped form the United Nations Children's Fund, also called UNICEF, which helps children all over the world.

Eleanor Roosevelt once spoke about how people express their thoughts through their actions. She said, "One's philosophy is not best expressed in words; it is expressed in the choices one makes...and the choices we make are ultimately our responsibility."

Your choices come from your thoughts. During that small moment between a choice and your decision, you think about your options. You can make better decisions by realizing the importance of these thoughts and the way your decision may affect other people around you. Also know that you're responsible for the results of your decisions, so whether they are positive or negative, you must live with the outcomes.

Today, make positive choices that demonstrate your power to make the world a better place.

Opportunities Follow Hard Work
Shelby Steele

Author Shelby Steele once wrote, "Opportunity follows struggles. It follows effort. It follows hard work. It doesn't come before."

Do you ever feel like new assignments or projects that are too hard aren't worth doing? If you do, remember that effort and hard work lead you closer to success. In fact, if you don't work hard, you probably won't have any new opportunities or successes.

Success is similar to the feeling you get when you shoot more and more baskets – your basketball skills improve consistently and your attitude about your skills becomes more positive. The more you practice, the better you get – even if you miss more shots than you'd like in the beginning as you develop your skills.

Even when things get very difficult, the successes and opportunities you'll find are well worth the struggle.

Dare to Fail Greatly

Robert F. Kennedy

How do people break records and become the best? Well, Robert F. Kennedy said, "Only those who dare to fail greatly can ever achieve greatly."

To be the best at something, you need to try to do it better than anyone else ever has. This means you must be motivated to use your skills in amazing new ways. You must commit to try your best and keep practicing until you improve. For example, if you are good at spelling, you could practice by trying to spell harder and harder words. Eventually, you may make it into the spelling bee and possibly win first place. Even if you don't win the first time you participate, the practice will help you get better.

People who want to do amazing things have to face the possibility of failure and making mistakes. Mistakes are part of getting better. If you dare to fail at something, you also dare to achieve something wonderful.

Focus on the Future

Alan Cohen

Negative thoughts about something that happened in the past will only make you feel bad. So instead, spend your time looking forward to great things in your future.

Alan Cohen once wrote, "Focus on what you are moving toward rather than what you are leaving behind." So if you have a problem, you should think about the solution. And when something bad happens, think of ways to prevent it from happening again. For example, say you get a low score on a test or assignment. Rather than feeling frustrated by your mistake, try channeling your energy and studying harder for the next time.

By doing this, you can forget the mistakes from the past and focus on better results in the future. By thinking about good things to come, your brain will think of ways to make these thoughts come true.

If Others Can, You Can Too

Abraham Lincoln

Why do some people receive good grades and others don't? The amount of effort that each student puts into his or her projects, tests, and assignments results in good or bad grades. So if you put a huge amount of effort into your work, you'll get higher scores. But on the other hand, if you don't put any effort at all into your work, then your scores will be lower.

Abraham Lincoln wrote, "That some have succeeded greatly is proof that others can as well." So if one of your classmates can get an A+, then you can get an A+ too.

Successful students think about how much they will study as soon as they get home. They also look for ways they can review their work, find mistakes, and make it better. These successful students don't feel good about their work until they have done their best.

You can earn the best grades in the whole class by putting in the largest amount of effort. The success of others proves it.

Try New Things
Dave Weinbaum

Dave Weinbaum once said, "The secret of a rich life is to have more beginnings than endings."

Every time you begin something new, you have new experiences and feelings. Lots of beginnings help you understand and know more about the world. With so much to learn, there's no time for anyone to waste with boredom. And anyone who refuses to learn new things robs himself of an exciting, rich life.

Begin something new and exciting today. Join a new club, read a new book, or make a new friend. Take advantage of all the opportunities that are around you every day.

Excellence is a Gradual Result
Pat Riley

Growth usually occurs gradually. As you grow, you don't feel each growth spurt as it happens. Instead growth suddenly becomes apparent when your clothes don't fit any longer, or you can reach things that were previously un-reachable.

Improvement is the same way; it occurs gradually. So as you learn new things, you must make small improvements over time to see results. It is far easier to learn new material gradually, than to cram a large amount of information at the last minute. Those who concentrate on improving each day will see great results over time.

Basketball coach and author Pat Riley once wrote, "Excellence is the gradual result of always wanting to do better."

Excellence is not seen after one great effort, but through incremental steps. Hard work, practice with feedback from teachers and mentors, and relentless focus on improvement, all become habits over time. Excellence training can become a normal part of your day if you teach yourself to focus and expect to work hard.

Mistakes Move You Closer to Success
Thomas Edison

The great inventor Thomas Edison never gave up trying new things. He lived from 1847 to 1931 and is responsible for the incandescent light bulb, the phonograph, and the motion picture camera. While it's no fun to make mistakes, every mistake you make gets you closer to your next success.

Edison once said, "People are not remembered by how few times they fail, but how often they succeed."

Don't worry about making mistakes. Everyone does it, even your parents and teachers. If you want to have great success and do amazing things, you must be willing to take risks and get things wrong once in a while.

You Become What You Think About

Napoleon Hill

Author Napoleon Hill once wrote about the "strangest secret." This secret was: "You become what you think about." So if you think about success, and picture yourself doing your work and enjoying it, then you will be a great success. But if you picture yourself failing, then your mind will lead you towards failure and retreat.

Did you know that some people actually tell themselves they won't succeed? Telling yourself things in this manner is called "self-talk." It is the voice in your mind that tells you positive or negative things. Many people make the mistake of thinking problems are too hard for them to solve. This makes them think they cannot accomplish very much, and they don't try.

The trick is to fill your mind with thoughts, pictures, and ideas about reaching your goals. When you work in class, you must tell yourself you can complete the assignment. Tell yourself to focus, pay close attention, and try your best. Tell yourself that you are a success, and you will be a success.

Rewards Are Proportionate to Effort
Earl Nightingale

If you don't try you won't succeed, and great success comes when you put in a lot of effort.

Author Earl Nightingale once wrote, "We will receive not what we idly wish for but what we justly earn. Our rewards will always be in exact proportion to our service."

You earn your success by the amount of effort you apply. Lots of effort will always bring you lots of success. If you wish for something to come true, it probably will never happen unless you take action to achieve it. People earn their success. You have to develop your skills and demonstrate the things you wish for through your actions. Success is the end result of great effort.

Hold Yourself Accountable
Henry Ward Beecher

Henry Ward Beecher was a lecturer, journalist, and preacher who lived from 1813 to 1887. He attracted thousands of people by his speeches, and he believed that people could accomplish their best when they expected themselves to do amazing things.

He said, "Hold yourself to a higher standard than anybody expects of you. Never excuse yourself."

You can make yourself do more than your family, teachers, or friends ask you to do. Don't do less than you are asked, but challenge yourself to do more. And don't allow yourself to make excuses for under-achievement. If you hold yourself to a higher standard you will be pleased at the progress you will make.

Actions Make a Reputation
Henry Ford

Henry Ford once said, "You can't build a reputation on what you are going to do." Henry Ford tried new things and understood that people remembered him for the things he worked on. Now he is remembered for making cars.

People know you by the things you've done, not by the things you thought about doing. The actions you take show your intentions. If your thoughts say you will do good things but you never actually do them, no one will know. So if doing good things matters to you, show this through your actions.

We Are What We Expect

Orison Swett Marden

Orison Swett Marden was a popular author in the early 1900s and founder of *Success* magazine. He once said, "We cannot rise higher than our thought of ourselves."

This means that we cannot do better than what we expect of ourselves. Everyone who wants to do amazing things needs to believe that he or she can do it. So today, think about what amazing things you'd like to do and imagine yourself doing them. Then, figure out what actions you can take now to get ready and get started. When you expect yourself to do great things, you will be successful.

Small Opportunities Lead to Great Accomplishments
Og Mandino

Author Og Mandino wrote, "Opportunities, many times, are so small that we glimpse them not and yet they are often the seeds of great enterprises. Opportunities are also everywhere and so you must always let your hook be hanging. When you least expect it, a great fish will swim by."

Did you know that you have 365 opportunities each year to do something amazing? Every morning when you rise out of bed, you are given the chance to take a step closer to your goals. Start today by deciding what you'd like to do or how you'd like to improve. Make a list of things you can do to improve your skills and start immediately since opportunities are all around us.

If you tried every day to train to be a great athlete or to learn another language, you would see a big difference over a short period of time. If you want to write a book, you could write a few sentences every day and revise your work as you go. You would have an impressive book by the end of the year.

Try every day to gain the skills you need to reach your goals. When you do, you'll achieve great success, one small step at a time.

Expect a Lot of Yourself

Earl Nightingale

Everyone harbors greatness within them, and everyone is special in some way. Sometimes that means you do very well in a particular area, but not so well in another. For example, you might be great in reading and writing, but not so good when it comes to physical education. However, don't think that great success is impossible just because you're not great at everything.

Many famous people had problems learning, but ended up being very successful. For example, Whoopi Goldberg had a learning disability that made her school work difficult, and Tom Cruise had a really hard time with reading. However, both were able to do amazing things with their lives. Everyone can do amazing things if they expect a lot of themselves.

Author Earl Nightingale wrote, "We tend to live up to our expectations."

Today, think about what great expectations you can hold for yourself. Understand that you can do amazing things, no matter what obstacles you face, because there is greatness in you.

Positive Friendships Help You Become Great
Mark Twain

Positive people make you feel better about yourself and more confident that you can meet your goals. Mark Twain once wrote, "Keep away from people who try to belittle your ambitions. Small people always do that, but the really great make you feel that you, too, can become great."

Make friends that encourage you to do good things, and be positive about other people's goals. True friends help each other get better and better. When you surround yourself with great friends, you'll always have the support and motivation to reach the goals you set.

Your Thoughts Control Your Effort
Andrew Hill

A ndrew Hill played basketball for Coach John Wooden at UCLA. In his book *Be Quick But Don't Hurry*, Andrew Hill described the lessons he learned from Coach Wooden. One of the main lessons he learned was that thoughts control effort.

Andrew Hill wrote, "Effort is internal and is completely within your control."

No matter what other people think, do, or say, they do not control how much you try. Your effort is up to you.

Today, focus on doing your very best work no matter what happens around you, and see just how successful you can be.

Friends Influence You
Proverb

According to the old proverb, "A man is known by the company he keeps."

Choose to be around those who do good things, because you cannot be totally successful alone. You need other people to teach you, help you, encourage you, and give you advice. These people are your friends, family members, and teachers who remind you that you can do great things.

True friends encourage others to make good choices. If you spend time with people who do bad things, you will learn to do similar things as well. Instead, choose to be around people who are positive and willing to help you.

ARISTOTLE AND HIS PUPIL, ALEXANDER.

Everyone Has Potential

Aristotle

A ristotle once said, "Each human being is bred with a unique set of potentials that yearn to be fulfilled as surely as the acorn yearns to become the oak within it."

Every single person in the world has a unique set of talents, abilities, and interests. Activities that involve a person's strengths tend to be easy and enjoyable for that person. They like getting better and better at activities they enjoy doing.

Take every chance you receive to learn new skills. You can do amazing things you never thought possible. Discovering new talents can be more fun than you ever imagined. Just as a seed has the power to ultimately become something greater, people have the same sense of future growth within them. You have great potential within you and you probably know deep down you can be, do, or have anything that you want in life. The secret of success lies within you – starting with your thoughts, followed by the actions and effort that lead you to reaching your potential.

Try Your Best
Michael Jordan

Michael Jordan was cut from his high school basketball team, but he never doubted his goal. He once said, "I can accept failure, but I can't accept not trying."

When you are not allowed to continue with a team, you might doubt whether or not you are a good player. But, like Michael Jordan did, you should see setbacks as signs that you need to try harder to achieve your goals.

Be ready to fail every time you try something, but remember that every failure brings you closer to your next success. Today, try your best to overcome all the challenges you face.

Effort Helps Your Immune System
Norman Cousins

Your body's immune system keeps you healthy and feeling good. The immune system stays strong if you eat healthy food, get enough rest, and feel good about yourself.

Norman Cousins once wrote, "Hope, purpose, and determination are not merely mental states. They have electrochemical connections that affect the immune system."

This means that positive people who have high hopes and want to work hard help their immune systems stay healthy. Today, do your best on every assignment and feel good about working hard, because great effort will help your immune system keep you healthy.

Perfect Practice Makes Perfect

John Wooden

You cannot learn everything you need to know on your own. You need help from experienced people to give you the information you need to improve.

UCLA basketball coach John Wooden taught his players, "Practice doesn't make perfect; only perfect practice makes perfect."

If you practice something without instruction and guidance, you may be practicing incorrectly. This is why your teachers work so hard to give you feedback on your work and help you improve. Remember to appreciate the advice you receive from teachers and others, because it helps improve your skills.

Project Into the Future
Bob Proctor

Author Bob Proctor said, "All of the great achievers of the past have been visionary figures; they were men and women who projected into the future. They thought of what could be, rather than what already was, and then they moved themselves into action, to bring these things into fruition."

When you dream about the future, make your dreams big. The secret to doing the amazing and the incredible is having a fantastic dream about the future. Once you have an amazing dream in mind, think about what you have to do to make it happen. Write down the details. What do you have to study? What skills do you need to build? Who do you need to know to get the help you will need?

By creating an amazing future in your mind and working towards it, your dreams can come true.

Astonish Yourself
Thomas Edison

You can be anything you want to be in life if you put in the effort. Once you decide you'd like to become a doctor, teacher, artist, sports figure, member of the fire department, or anything else, you can make it happen. The first part is you have to believe you can do it.

Thomas Edison once said, "If we did all the things we are capable of doing, we would literally astonish ourselves."

If your mind tells you that you cannot do something, you won't feel like doing the necessary work to succeed. Instead, fill your mind with positive messages. You possess the ability to learn any skill you need to do amazing things with your life.

Look for the Positive

Sir John Lubbock

R esearchers have found that people think approximately 50,000 thoughts each day. These thoughts can be positive or negative, but only you choose how you think about things that happen to you.

Sir John Lubbock once said, "What we see depends mainly on what we look for."

Always try to see the positive side of the things that happen around you. By doing so, you will find many people who do great things all around you. And if you choose to think positively, you can be one of those people who achieve great things.

Plant Seeds of Opportunity Daily
Robert Louis Stevenson

R obert Louis Stevenson, who lived from 1850 to 1894, was an author of many popular books, including *Treasure Island*. He wrote, "Don't judge each day by the harvest you reap, but by the seed you plant."

Each day you have many opportunities to do great things, but do not expect success to happen all in one day. Just like you need to learn to add and subtract before you can learn to multiply and divide, it is unrealistic to think that anyone can solve complex math problems without knowing the simple basics. Each day is a building block that leads you to future success and greater challenges. Apply yourself to strengthen your foundation and consider each day as a chance to learn new ideas that will lead you to greater success in the future.

No Excuses

Mary Frances Berry

Excuses are easy to find when you don't feel like doing something. But you need to force yourself to do what you don't want to do. One way to get yourself going is to consider the positive reasons for working hard.

Mary Frances Berry once said, "Some men have thousands of reasons why they cannot do what they want to, when all they need is one reason why they can."

You feel more motivated to work hard when you think of good reasons for doing so. Today, think of how much you can learn if you apply yourself. By giving your best effort, you will see yourself get better and better.

Sail, Don't Drift

Oliver Wendell Holmes

Oliver Wendell Holmes lived from 1809 to 1894. He was a doctor, as well as an author whose poems and essays appeared in many magazines and newspapers.

Oliver Wendell Holmes wrote, "I find the great thing in this world is not so much where we stand, as in what direction we are moving: To reach the port of heaven, we must sail sometimes with wind and sometimes against it, but we must sail, and not drift, nor lie at anchor."

When pursuing any goal, the important thing is to keep moving. When sailing you can encounter all sorts of obstacles, such as dangerous changes in the wind or unsafe waters. Unexpected events will always stand in the way of your goals. The crucial thing to remember is to take actions that move you in the direction of your goals, even when obstacles arise.

Your Future Results From Daily Effort
Mike Murdock

Every day you get chances to do things that make you smarter. If you focus your day on improving your skills, you will naturally move yourself closer to success.

Author Mike Murdock once said, "The secret of your future is hidden in your daily routine."

Your future depends on how hard you work daily on areas where you need to improve. For example, if you want to be a better skateboarder, plan time for practice every day. Or if you want to be a better reader, add a specific amount of quiet reading time to your daily routine.

Today, choose an area where you'd like to improve, think of things you can do to strengthen key skills in that area, and then get started.

Expect Challenges
Johann Wolfgang von Goethe

German philosopher Johann Wolfgang von Goethe once wrote, "Everything is hard before it is easy." Expect your work to become more challenging every day. As the work becomes harder, you must learn to listen closely to directions and the advice you are given. When you work hard every day, you develop positive habits.

The habits of listening closely and working hard become automatic if you practice them each day. When your teacher explains new things, listen closely to what he or she says, and try your best on every assignment. These behaviors become automatic and easy over time. If you do these things every day, getting your work done will become easier than it has ever been in the past.

Light Another Candle
James Keller

Is it difficult to make the world a better place? No. In fact, it is very simple. You can make the world a better place simply by being kind to other people. By talking to others about positive things, you help others to think in a positive way.

Author James Keller once wrote, "A candle loses nothing by lighting another candle."

You can share your brightness with others by being kind and positive. This means not following other people's bad examples. Instead, set a good example by doing good things and you will make the world a better place, one person at a time.

Untapped Potential
Brian Tracy

Researchers from the Stanford University Brain Institute study how much people use their brains. These researchers say that most people only use about two percent of their potential. This means that we don't use about ninety-eight percent of our brain. Each person has an abundance of abilities and possibilities, ninety-eight percent of which are untapped.

Author Brian Tracy wrote, "The potential of the average person is like a huge ocean un-sailed, a new continent unexplored, a world of possibilities waiting to be released and channeled toward some great good."

Through effort you can discover these uncharted waters that exist inside you. Nothing is too hard. Nothing is impossible. But you cannot copy what unsuccessful people do and expect to be successful. If you choose not to listen and not to work, you cannot be a success. Today, put forth all the effort you can to be a great success because your brain is able to do more than you can imagine.

Overcoming Obstacles
Helen Keller

Helen Keller lived from 1880 to 1968. When she was less than two years old, she became very ill. The illness resulted in Helen becoming blind and deaf. Through the help of her teacher, Anne Sullivan, she was able to become independent and went on to help other people with disabilities.

Helen Keller once wrote, "Keep your face to the sunshine and you cannot see the shadow."

Despite being unable to see, hear, or speak, Helen Keller overcame many obstacles. She accomplished this largely by finding value in helping others who had problems similar to her own. Today, if you find a problem or difficulty, look for a solution outside yourself. Often the best solutions come from doing positive things for others.

Dreams Lead to Flight
Langston Hughes

Poet Langston Hughes wrote,

"Hold fast to dreams
for if dreams die,
life is a broken winged bird
that cannot fly."

Without dreams and goals for the future, people miss out on the fun and excitement of planning and working towards something amazing. True happiness comes from the adventure of working towards something new. Today, think about your dreams and what you need to do to make them happen, but don't forget to enjoy the journey.

Get Ready for Opportunities
Abraham Lincoln

A braham Lincoln once said, "I prepare and someday my chance will come." Lincoln worked incredibly hard to learn new things. He persisted in learning, even while working on a farm, tending a store at New Salem, Illinois, and many other jobs. His thinking was to get his skills ready, because someday he would put them to good use.

If Abraham Lincoln had chosen not to study, he would never have been successful later as a lawyer, legislator, or President. Similarly, you should take the same attitude by preparing yourself for the future through hard work and studies today. These efforts will prepare you for wonderful opportunities that will arise later in your life.

Determination and Effort
Gary Player

Gary Player is a famous professional golfer who was born in South Africa in 1935. After dominating golf in South Africa, he traveled to England where he was told he did not have the skills to become a successful golfer and should change careers.

This challenge made Player even more determined. He practiced and prepared all the time. He followed an intense fitness routine that made him fitter than men far younger than he. He continued playing and winning in Europe and the United States.

Gary Player once said, "The harder you work, the luckier you get."

Gary Player was successful because he was determined to reach his goals and worked hard. The same can happen to you if you are determined to work hard each day. Your amount of daily effort will determine how successful you become, despite what anyone tells you.

Trustworthiness
Thomas Jefferson

People who are honest are trustworthy and dependable. They are the people you can rely on for help and support, and they are the people you should admire. Most important, honest and trustworthy people do not lie about anything, even when it seems like the easiest way to overcome obstacles.

Thomas Jefferson wrote, "Honesty is the first chapter in the book of wisdom." With that in mind, if you want to make and keep friends, if you want to be successful at school or home, and if you want to be someone who receives important responsibilities, you must be honest.

When other people can trust you, they are confident that you will do what you say you will do. They will trust you with their thoughts and feelings, and they will know they can rely on you. Trustworthiness is one of the many keys to your future success.

Don't Procrastinate
Benjamin Franklin

Procrastination means putting things off until the last minute. For example, when you put off studying for an important test until the night before, that's procrastinating. And those of you who have procrastinated your schoolwork in the past, know that it doesn't always yield the best results. You can never get back time you have wasted, so you should take advantage of every moment to focus on what is most important.

Benjamin Franklin once said, "Never leave till tomorrow what you can do today." The most important thing to do at each moment depends on directions and assignments your teacher gives you. So when you have an important assignment, daydreaming or talking to someone around you instead of listening to directions won't help you get it done. And your work will never get done, unless you do it. Focus on getting the most important assignments done, and when you have finished, you can relax and enjoy the feeling of success.

Opportunities in Difficulties

Sir Winston Churchill

Pessimists are people who identify the negative aspects of all situations, while optimists are people who identify the positive aspects of all situations. Sir Winston Churchill was an optimist who lived from 1874 until 1965. He was a soldier, leader, writer, artist, and statesman; and in 1940 he became Prime Minister of Great Britain.

Churchill once wrote, "A pessimist sees the difficulty in every opportunity; an optimist sees the opportunity in every difficulty." This means that the way you think about things has a huge impact on the actions you take.

For example, if you come to a difficult math problem with a pessimistic outlook, then you'll likely give up and skip the problem. But with an optimistic outlook, you'll see the difficult problem as an opportunity to learn, and your determination will lead to success.

Today, embrace an optimistic outlook and seek out opportunities to work hard and learn new things. These challenges are true learning opportunities.

Positive Thinking
Warren Buffett

Too many people tell themselves negative things all day long. They think they won't get good grades, or they won't pass the test, or they won't win. But this is a mistake because if you tell yourself you cannot do something, your brain believes it.

Businessman Warren Buffett said, "If you think you're going to succeed, you will." So instead of telling yourself all the things you can't do, tell yourself you can do amazing things and be a great success. Your brain will work hard to make sure these thoughts come true.

Approach your new challenges with confidence. Tell yourself that you will be successful and that you can learn anything presented to you, because as long as you believe it, you can achieve it.

We Are Here to Help Each Other

Jeff Warner

Jeff Warner once said, "We are not put on this earth for ourselves, but are placed here for each other. If you are there always for others, then in time of need, someone will be there for you."

Things work naturally this way. For example, if you plant a tree and water it, the tree will grow. Your good deed caused something good to happen in that tree. Then the tree can provide you and others with shade and fruit.

You should never do something good with the expectation of receiving some payment or benefit from your efforts. People naturally want to respond to good deeds by doing good deeds in return. Those who are generous without any expectations will receive generosity from other people. But anyone who is mean and angry only receives anger from others.

Today, do good things for others because you want to make a difference. If you do things without expecting anything in return, you will end up making more friends and having more people willing to help than you can imagine.

Creative People Enjoy Finding Improvement
Joseph Chilton Pierce

Author Joseph Chilton Pierce once wrote, "To live a creative life, we must lose our fear of being wrong." In other words, you can create a great painting or poem, but usually it is carefully thought out and drafted in advance. To successfully be creative you must work with drafts, sketches, and revisions.

Creative people don't worry about what the first draft looks like. They don't have any fear about revising their work to improve it. Creative people enjoy finding areas of improvement and try many times to get things just right. The greatest final product does not often happen the first time. Creative minds feel better about works they have fixed over time than works they've only attempted once.

Today, make sure to revise your work and make it better. Look for improvement and enjoy finding your own mistakes. If you do, you'll be surprised at how creative you really are.

Why Not?

George Bernard Shaw

An author named George Bernard Shaw wrote, "You see things that are and say, 'Why?' But I dream things that never were and say, 'Why not?'"

Dreams are your imagination at work, inventing new possibilities. Some of the greatest innovators asked "why not?" of their dreams and imaginations and made the world better for everyone.

There is no end to the amazing possibilities you can create through your imagination. The world would not be as exciting if there weren't new things being created each day.

You also have the power to create new, innovative, and exciting things that will benefit others. The power rests inside your brain, just waiting for you to activate new possibilities. All you have to do is ask yourself, "Why not?"

Use Every Opportunity to Show Kindness
William Penn

K indness means giving your time and energy to assist someone who can use your help, without expecting anything in return. William Penn once wrote, "I expect to pass through life but once. If, therefore, there be any kindness I can show, or any good thing I can do to any fellow being, let me do it now, for I shall not pass this way again."

He means that if you come across someone in need of kindness, you should take advantage of the chance to help them because that opportunity may not exist later. Be kind to others at every opportunity. Kind acts not only make you feel better about yourself because you are helping someone, but they also leave that person in a better place.

For example, think about how you feel when someone is nice to you out of their own kindness. When someone is nice to you, it is natural for you to want to be nice to that person and other people you encounter. Kindness has a tendency to rub off on others, so you shouldn't pass up the opportunity to spread it around. Take the time today to do something good for someone else without expecting anything from them in return.

Persistence

William Feather

When you work on a problem with other people, why does one person usually get the answer before all the others do? Is it because that person was the last one to give up?

Author and publisher William Feather once said, "Success seems to be largely a matter of hanging on after others have let go."

If a problem is very difficult, most people tend to give up. But only the person who is most persistent will be the successful one to discover the solution. Today, remain focused on the project or assignment you are working on, and be the one who is persistent even when others have given up.

Everything Big Starts With One Small Action
Amanda Cross

A manda Cross is an author who wrote many, many long mystery books. You may be wondering how she ever approached such big projects. She once wrote, "You decide to do something, perform one small action, and suddenly it's a tide, the momentum is going and there's no possibility of turning back. Somehow, even though you thought you foresaw all that would happen, you didn't know the pace would pick up so."

The key to accomplishing a big project is simply getting started. And many times, getting started is the hardest part. For some people, just typing a few lines on a computer or writing a few words on paper is enough to get them started on a wonderful 300 page novel. So if you just start with a small part of a large assignment, the momentum will pick up and you will probably find yourself doing more than you thought you could.

Note: The name, "Amanda Cross," has appeared on many mystery books. But this name is actually a pseudonym for Carolyn Heilbrun. This means Carolyn Heilbrun wrote the books, but preferred to use another name as the author.

Effort is its Own Reward

Ralph Waldo Emerson

When you are part of a team, you have important work to do. Don't say you're part of a team if you will not help. Each participant has a variety of skills and should use those skills to accomplish the team's goals. Individual credit doesn't happen because the efforts of the entire team are judged. If the best possible effort is given by all members of the team, then all team members can feel the same great feeling of accomplishment.

Ralph Waldo Emerson once wrote, "The reward of a thing well done is having done it."

Your reward for great participation with your group is the completion of the project to the best of the group's ability. If you choose not to participate, you are letting down your friends as well as yourself. If everyone on the team gives their best effort, your group will earn the success they deserve.

Citizenship
Jawaharlal Nehru

Jawaharlal Nehru lived from 1889 to 1964, and he served as prime minister of India from 1947 to 1964.

Jawaharlal Nehru once said, "Citizenship consists in the service of country."

Being a good citizen involves doing good things for others. Serving your country can involve helping those who need help and following established laws and rules. On school campuses, many volunteer opportunities exist, such as running for student council or organizing a campus clean-up. As good student citizens, you can participate in sports, music, and other extracurricular activities. These activities promote a sense of community at the school that comes from the efforts of people who unite to do extra.

You can show you know what it means to be a good citizen by following the rules and cooperating with others.

Make Opportunities

Francis Bacon

When you encounter a challenge, how do you react? Do you back away from it? Or do you look at it as a wonderful opportunity to grow? Even if it's scary because it's new, you can make the most of what happens to you.

Francis Bacon once said, "A wise man will make more opportunities than he finds."

This means that a wise person will make opportunities or think of new ways to help, and then take the initiative to pursue them. Someone who finds opportunities responds to suggestions made by their teachers, family members, and friends. You can start by making a list of new challenges and asking others for input on how you can get started.

You can choose to give a great effort or to hold back. In the end, every person decides how he or she responds to new opportunities. If you really want to challenge yourself, you will look for new opportunities whenever possible by trying new things.

Opportunities for Learning
Albert Einstein

People naturally like to do things that come easy to them, and avoid things that are more difficult. But that's because they fail to see the opportunity in their challenges. Whenever you are stuck in the middle of a difficult assignment, do you look at that moment as an opportunity for learning?

Albert Einstein once said, "In the middle of difficulty lies opportunity." This means that we learn the most from the challenges we face.

You won't find many opportunities if you keep avoiding challenges and doing things that are remarkably easy for you. Look for challenges that force you to develop your skills and you will find opportunities.

Do More Than Expected

Saint Francis of Assisi

When you exceed expectations, you do more. You go beyond what you are told to do. In school, exceeding expectations may mean earning an "A" in every class, or doing more research than is required for a particular project. Regardless of what expectations are held for any project, it is always possible to do more.

Saint Francis of Assisi said, "Start by doing what is necessary; then do what's possible; and suddenly you are doing the impossible."

By doing what is possible, not just what is necessary, you will accomplish more than what is expected of you. Students who put extra effort into their studies can accomplish amazing things. When you extend yourself to accomplish more, little by little you can achieve what others think is impossible.

Look Where You Want to Go
Bob Ernst

People who don't think about goals tend to think about what makes them happy right now. If you're happy right now by doing very little, how does that impact your future? Successful people think about how their actions in the present can help or hurt them in the future. If you maintain focus on your goals, you will take actions that help you achieve your goals.

Bob Ernst once wrote, "Never look where you're going. Always look where you want to go."

Do things with your time that connect to where you want to go. If you want to be a doctor, spend time learning about health, fitness, and medicine. If you want to be an Olympic athlete, spend time training in the sport of your choice. By thinking about what you want to be in the future, you'll make better choices about how you spend your time today.

Success Involves Tenacity

Mary Kay Ash

You don't have to believe anyone who tells you that you cannot achieve something great. You can be, do, or have anything you want in life. But you need to work hard until you become the person you set out to be.

Mary Kay Ash once said, "It never occurred to me that I couldn't do it. I always knew that if I worked hard enough, I could."

Hard work involves tenacity. If you are tenacious, you don't give up even when others say negative things about your goals. Today, keep working hard and believe that you can achieve your goals because you are willing to put in the effort.

Paying Attention Enhances Productivity

Tom Peters

A ttention is defined as: "Concentration of the mental powers upon an object."

You use attention any time you focus your thoughts on something. Focusing your attention also focuses your creative energy, or the part of your mind that energizes you to take action. For example, if you think about playing a game or calling a friend on the telephone, then your creative energy helps you do what you are thinking about. It makes you productive.

Author Tom Peters says, "The simple act of paying positive attention to people has a great deal to do with productivity."

Pay attention to details, and think about an area where you'd like to improve. Then let your creative energy motivate you to use the details and complete great projects. If you focus your attention on improvement, you'll find that sooner or later your creative energy will help you produce results.

Potential in Everyone

Paul Bauer

A tiny seed needs to be planted and cared for before it can become a wonderful, strong tree. A seed is only the beginning of an amazing journey that involves change and transformation.

Paul Bauer wrote, "In each of you, there is a seed…a seed of vast potential."

Inside every person lies the potential for many new beginnings. You transform yourself by learning new skills, reading books, and making new friends. Every day presents opportunities for you to learn and grow. Today, remember that inside you exists a seed of vast potential for greatness.

Take Action
Peter Nivio Zarlenga

Have you ever spent a lot of time worrying about a problem? Fear makes it easy to worry about problems, and fear also makes it easy to avoid doing something about problems.

Peter Nivio Zarlenga said, "Action conquers fear."

By taking action in the face of a problem, you alleviate your fears and feel better about yourself. You can worry for a long time about an upcoming test, but if you sit down and study you can build the confidence and knowledge required to do well on the test. If other people harass you or pressure you to do things you know are wrong, you can take positive action to conquer your fears, such as talking to an adult about the situation.

If you are concerned about any problem at school, take action, talk to an adult you trust, and brainstorm a solution to the problem.

It is Better to Be Prepared
Whitney Young Jr.

Your preparation is everything. Preparation requires effort and determination. Whenever you are in a classroom, reading a book, or working on a project, you are able to prepare yourself for bigger and more challenging opportunities.

Civil Rights leader, Whitney Young Jr., once said, "It is better to be prepared for an opportunity and not have one, than to have an opportunity and not be prepared."

If you choose not to use your time in class, you choose not to be prepared for future opportunities. Every chance you have to learn and improve your skills, take the time to give your best effort. By always doing your best, you will be ready for fantastic opportunities.

A Rich Tapestry
Maya Angelou

Do you make friends with people who do things differently? Whether their families eat foods that are new to you, or speak other languages, these are opportunities for you to learn new things that some may never experience for themselves. Be aware that you are very fortunate to know people who are different.

Author Maya Angelou wrote, "We all should know that diversity makes for a rich tapestry, and we must understand that all the threads of the tapestry are equal in value no matter what their color."

Making friends with people who are different from you can be a fun way to learn about different cultures and traditions. It's like being a part of a rainbow full of different colors, where no color is more important than other colors. The differences make the rainbow interesting.

Effort Comes From Within

Ralph Waldo Emerson

The way you look at challenges and the effort you give are important indicators of your future success. It matters more if you give a great effort today than if you failed yesterday. The ability to give a great effort is what lies within you.

Ralph Waldo Emerson wrote, "What lies behind us and what lies before us are tiny matters compared to what lies within us."

You may have experienced problems in the past, and you will definitely experience challenges in the future. But your effort level must remain strong in the face of challenges because the person who does not try is worse off than the person who fails. The person who doesn't try does not care enough to make an effort. If you make an effort to do something challenging, you can do great things even if you haven't been successful in the past.

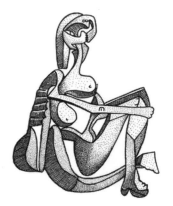

Work and Inspiration
Pablo Picasso

Do you ever find it difficult to start writing a story or a report for class? If you sit and spend too much time wondering what to write, then you'll never finish your first sentence. Actually, you become more creative and inspired after you have started. Once you begin writing, your brain thinks of more ideas.

The great artist Pablo Picasso said, "Inspiration exists, but it has to find us working."

Science books tell us that it takes ten units of energy to get something moving but one unit of energy to keep the object in motion. In other words, it is easier to keep going than it is to get started. So stop thinking and start writing. The best part is that once you have some good ideas, you can go back and make the entire written piece even better, and generate even more inspiration.

First a Dream
Carl Sandburg

Carl Sandburg was an American poet, historian, and novelist. He lived from 1878 to 1967, and won several Pulitzer Prizes for his books on Abraham Lincoln and his poetry.

Carl Sandburg wrote, "Nothing happens unless first a dream." In other words, to accomplish anything, first you must have the thought. Then you can take action to make your thought a reality, or you can choose to do nothing. All people are responsible for controlling their responses and for making choices about how they spend their time. Today, spend time thinking about what you would love to be, to do, or to have – then choose to make the effort to do whatever it takes to turn that dream into reality.

Actions Reveal Beliefs
Anatole France

A natole France was a French writer who won the Nobel Prize for Literature in 1921. He lived from 1844 to 1924.

Anatole France wrote, "It is by acts and not by ideas that people live."

You can have the best ideas in the world, but if you never act on your ideas, then no one will know how wonderful they are. Great ideas about doing good things are not enough. People know you by the things you do, not from the ideas you have. You are responsible for all of your actions. So choose to show your thoughts and beliefs through your actions. When you do, you can make the world a better place.

Do Your Best
George Halas

George Halas lived from 1895 to 1983. He was a football pioneer who was named the Most Valuable Player in the 1919 Rose Bowl, was a coach, and an owner of the Chicago Bears. He won eight NFL titles and was elected to the NFL Hall of Fame in 1963.

George Halas once said, "Nobody who ever gave his best regretted it."

What do you lose if you try your hardest? Most of the time, you lose nothing but you gain everything. In trying your hardest, you stretch your abilities to the limit, you learn new things, and you feel good about yourself. People who don't try their best, don't have the chance to feel great when they have improved. Today, do your best at something – you will not regret it.

A Problem is a Chance
Duke Ellington

Duke Ellington lived from 1899 to 1974. He led an orchestra, played piano, composed over 2,000 pieces of music, and has been called America's greatest composer. But Ellington didn't like piano lessons as a child. He became interested in piano when he was a teenager.

Duke Ellington once said, "A problem is a chance for you to do your best."

Even though he didn't like piano lessons, he did his best to play the piano when he was a teenager. He did his best and became one of the most honored musicians in our country. He was so honored that President Nixon threw his 70th birthday party at the White House. There Duke was awarded the Presidential Medal of Freedom. But if he gave up on the piano as a child, he would have never achieved such honors.

Today, whenever you face a problem, remember it's a chance to do your best and great honor will result from your efforts.

One Person Can Do Amazing Things

Pierre de Coubertin

Have you ever wanted to do something really important that people all over the world would enjoy? Pierre de Coubertin did exactly that. He was born in Paris, France in 1863. He loved history and often thought about why the French army had lost the battle with the Prussians in 1870. He found that the soldiers were out of shape and needed more training. Pierre was determined to make sure that didn't happen again, so he worked to involve children in sports and fitness. Through his work with schools, he started thinking about how great it would be to hold Olympic Games again as had been done centuries before in ancient times. He took action on his dreams, and in 1894 he formed a delegation of twelve countries willing to establish the International Olympic Committee.

To create the Olympic flag, an important symbol of the Games, Pierre de Coubertin said, "The six colours, including the white background, represent the colours of all the world's flags...this is a true international emblem."

By wanting to promote fitness, friendliness between countries, and the idea that people can train themselves to achieve amazing things, Pierre de Coubertin made an enormous difference in the world. If you have a great idea that will help others, don't give up – your idea can make a wonderful difference in the world.

Habits Are Strengthened Daily

Horace Mann

Horace Mann is often called "The Father of American Education." In 1837, as Secretary of Education, Mann worked to make sure public schools would be available to all. He established a set number of days students would attend school and also created programs where people could study to become teachers. He knew that studying each day was a powerful habit.

Horace Mann once wrote, "Habit is a cable; we weave a thread of it every day, and at last we can not break it."

Every day you can work to strengthen your habits to the point where they are unbreakable. If you do your best every day, giving a great effort becomes a habit. If you do special projects or read at specific times during the day, these become habits as well. When you reach this level, and hard work becomes a habit, it will actually feel strange to not give a great effort. Keep up the great work and you will develop fantastic habits that will make you more productive in your schoolwork.

Truth is Valuable

Mark Twain

Mark Twain once wrote, "Truth is the most valuable thing we have."

Trust is everything. People who are honest can be consistently trusted and given great responsibilities. Those who do not tell the truth may think they have an advantage for a moment. But in the end, most lies are discovered, and people will hesitate to trust someone who has lied in the past.

Today, and in the future, remember to tell the truth. When you are honest you help make relationships stronger, and make the world a more trustworthy place.

Dream Big Dreams
Johann Wolfgang von Goethe

The author Johann Wolfgang von Goethe once wrote, "Dream no small dreams for they have no power to move men."

People who dream are excited about doing new things, and come up with creative ways to reach these goals. Large dreams are the ideas that motivate people to do amazing things. They are the dreams, so big, that they are powerful enough to move men. Incredible dreams help people see that the impossible can sometimes be achieved.

Today, think about your big dreams, and find creative ways you and others can make these dreams come true.

Patience is a Protection
Leonardo da Vinci

Leonardo da Vinci was a famous architect, painter, designer, and writer. He did incredible things with his time. He also knew how important it is to be patient with projects, new ideas, and other people.

Da Vinci once wrote, "Patience serves as a protection against wrongs as clothes do against cold."

People who are patient are less likely to make large mistakes. Patient people don't do things out of anger or haste, but instead take their time to think about why things are happening around them. Today, remember to be patient, especially when things don't go very well. Patience will keep you from making mistakes.

Make Your Ideas Come Alive

Dr. Myron S. Allen

Dr. Myron S. Allen once said, "An idea in a cage is like a silver dollar buried in the ground. Both are safe, but neither produces anything."

If you keep your ideas to yourself and never do anything about them, they won't become reality. Think about your ideas, dreams, and goals and what you need to do to make them happen. Start working on the skills you need to make the dreams come true. If you work to develop an important skill each day, you will see a huge difference over a short period of time. But it all starts by figuring out the steps you need to take to make your ideas, dreams, and goals come true. Sharing your ideas with friends and family will help you brainstorm more possibilities for making your dreams become realities. By thinking about your ideas, talking about them, and building the skills you need, you are letting your ideas out of the cage and producing results.

Lying Leads to More Lies
Vaclav Havel

Vaclav Havel was elected President of Czechoslovakia in December of 1989, and later on he was also President of the Czech Republic.

Vaclav Havel once wrote, "Lying can never save us from another lie."

Once a person lies there will ultimately be other lies necessary to assist the first lie. You cannot get away with just one. Lying starts a cycle of lies that only gets worse as others ask questions. You may find yourself caught in an elaborate web of lies that can only end in disaster. Only telling the truth can save you from having to tell more lies.

Today, keep in mind that even the smallest, most innocent mistruth can lead to huge, more damaging lies.

The Power of Reading
Walt Disney

Walt Disney loved to read, and he knew how fun both fiction and non-fiction could be.

He said, "There is more treasure in books than in all the pirates' loot on Treasure Island...and best of all, you can enjoy these riches every day."

Reading can allow you to explore distant lands and exotic cultures any time you want. As long as you have a book, you can experience new worlds that you might never experience if you didn't read. Today, allow yourself to escape reality and explore your imagination by reading a new book.

The Universe Conspires With You

Paulo Coelho

A Brazilian writer named Paulo Coelho wrote, "When you want something, all the universe conspires in helping you to achieve it."

In everything you do throughout the day, if you keep your goals in mind, you will find opportunities to learn new things and meet people who can help you achieve these goals. You will discover so many opportunities that it will seem like all the knowledge and help you need is actually around you each day, ready to assist you in achieving great things.

When you visualize yourself achieving a goal, that image tells your brain that it is possible. Writing your goals on paper is an excellent way to form a picture of them in your mind. Then when you write down the necessary steps to make those goals come true, the road to fulfilling them becomes clear. The next step is to review your goals when you get up in the morning and before you go to sleep at night. Then throughout the day you will think about practicing your skills and talking to people who can help you achieve your dreams. This process of writing and reviewing your goals will help you keep in mind all that you have to do to achieve them.

Learn From Mistakes

George Bernard Shaw

L earning new things is important to help you prepare for new challenges; but people often avoid challenging tasks in fear of making mistakes.

George Bernard Shaw once wrote, "A life spent making mistakes is not only more honorable, but more useful than a life spent doing nothing."

Don't avoid difficult things because you're afraid to make mistakes. Making mistakes means that you're trying; and the more challenging your assignment, the more you stretch yourself to develop important skills. You should expect to make mistakes – that is how you know you continue to learn and stretch your abilities.

Obstacles Develop Achievement Muscles
Thomas Carlyle

For every good idea, there will be potential troubles and surprises that you might encounter. Whether you'd like to write a book, raise money for a charity, or do something wonderful for your family, there may be obstacles that get in the way every time you try something new or innovative.

Thomas Carlyle once wrote, "Nothing stops the man who desires to achieve. Every obstacle is simply a course to develop his achievement muscle. It's a strengthening of his powers of achievement."

Look at obstacles or problems as challenges that make you stronger, but don't let them stop you. Problems that get in the way only test your willingness to put in all your effort. Today, make sure to put all your effort into challenging assignments.

Stretching Your Abilities is Living
Karl Wallenda

Karl Wallenda was a circus acrobat famous for walking the tightrope. He also founded the Great Wallendas acrobatic troupe, which achieved fame in Europe for its four-man pyramid and for cycling on the high wire without a safety net.

Karl Wallenda said, "Being on the tightrope is living; everything else is waiting."

To walk the tightrope, you need to be able to focus on what you are doing and follow through on an exciting challenge. Choosing not to do something new that stretches your abilities is like sitting around waiting. Doing new things stretches your mind to be able to take on new challenges. Don't be frightened of trying new things. The confidence you need to be successful comes from taking on new challenges.

Enthusiasm Despite Failure
Sir Winston Churchill

Failure is part of learning. Making mistakes leads you to understand how to do things better and take on larger, more complex challenges. If you use the feedback you receive to improve, you don't have a reason to feel badly about making mistakes. Mistakes are opportunities to learn and improve. You can move directly to the next challenge with the same excitement about learning.

Sir Winston Churchill said, "Success is the ability to go from one failure to another with no loss of enthusiasm."

When you find you have made mistakes, use that as a chance to improve your skills. Be excited that you are learning and improving. Over time, you will be able to take on larger and larger challenges because your skills keep growing and growing.

Be Willing to Help One Another
Sallust

Sallust was a Roman historian who lived from 86-34BC. His writings were different from those of previous historians because he tried to explain how events were connected rather than just telling what happened. In particular, Sallust recognized what made groups of people successful.

Sallust wrote, "By union the smallest states thrive. By discord the greatest are destroyed."

In other words, a small group can be mighty if they are united towards a common purpose. A small group interested in helping one another is far more powerful than a large group who fights with one another. Even the greatest cluster of friends can be destroyed through disagreement.

Classes are like that too. The most memorable, wonderful experiences come when a group of people loves helping one another. Today, make sure to be a part of a group of people willing to help one another, rather than fight with each other. If you are one of those helpful people, your group will have positive results.

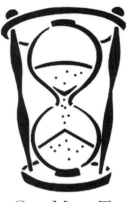

One More Try

William Strong

Does it ever feel like you fail every time you try something new? Some tasks and activities are very difficult and demand that you take the time to learn the necessary skills. For example, people are rarely able to ride a bicycle or swim well the first time they try. But what happens if the person only tries to swim once and then gives up?

William Strong once said, "The only time you don't fail is the last time you try anything – and it works."

So even after numerous failures, success in anything you try could possibly result from just one more attempt. For example, imagine your favorite sports figure or movie star. What if that person didn't keep trying to do what they love doing? Well for one thing, they wouldn't be famous because they would never have found success.

As you try new things, you'll inevitably fail once in a while. But remember that the next time you try could be the start of your next great success.

Actions Reveal Thoughts
John Locke

John Locke was born in England in 1632. He studied medicine in school, but even after graduating college he continued to study and read all the time. He also published his views on government and the natural rights of people.

Locke once wrote, "I have always thought the actions of men the best interpreters of their thoughts."

He believed that people show their thoughts through their actions. For example, even if someone says they think lying or stealing is wrong, they must show this belief through their actions. So this person may demonstrate their belief by being honest and truthful.

What do you believe? Today, show others what you think is important through your actions. Through positive actions you can make the world a better place.

PLATO.

Never Discourage Anyone
Plato

How do you feel when someone tells you you've done a great job on something? You probably feel motivated to keep going and proud of yourself because positive comments make people feel good inside. Positive words encourage positive actions, and people need encouragement all the time to keep up their motivation to work hard and help others.

The philosopher Plato once said, "Never discourage anyone...who continually makes progress, no matter how slow."

You know that in learning a new skill, it takes time and practice to make progress. Sometimes progress can take a long time. If you know someone who is trying to learn something new and making progress, even slow progress, continue to encourage them with positive words.

Conquer Your Thoughts
Sir Edmund Hillary

Sir Edmund Hillary and Tenzing Norgay were the first climbers to reach the top of Mount Everest. No one else had done it prior to their achievement in 1953. But within a few decades, hundreds of other people from many nations would climb Everest too.

Sir Edmund Hillary once said, "It is not the mountain we conquer but ourselves."

Before Hillary and Norgay, people had believed it was impossible to get to the top of Mount Everest. They thought it was too tall and too dangerous for anyone to show the discipline to make it to the top. But Sir Edmund Hillary and Tenzing Norgay told themselves it was not impossible. They conquered their own thoughts and doubts, and kept working towards a goal no one had yet achieved.

By telling yourself you can do something incredible and overcoming your own doubts, you can make unbelievable things happen.

Do With All Your Might
Marcus Tullius Cicero

Marcus Tullius Cicero was a philosopher, poet, lawyer, and statesman who lived from 106 BC to 43 BC. His teachings influenced the thinking of many people around him, and he was known as a defender of liberty and the sharing of new ideas. For example, he shared the innovative ideas of the Greeks with the Romans and other civilizations.

Cicero once said, "Whatever you do, do with all your might."

He felt it was important to discuss new ideas and to encourage people to speak their minds. In his life, he pursued these beliefs with all his might even though these beliefs sometimes meant he himself would be unpopular.

If you truly believe in something, why would you pursue it without really trying? As Cicero knew, the secret of doing a great job and accomplishing new things is giving a great effort. In everything you try, the amount of effort you put forth will be clearly seen in your results.

Remind Yourself of What You Do Right

Brian Koslow

The thoughts you have throughout the day have tremendous impact on the way you feel and on what you accomplish. Therefore, your mental energy should never be wasted by telling yourself you cannot get things done or that you'll never learn the material you are studying.

Author Brian Koslow once wrote, "To accomplish more, redirect your mental energy by continuously reminding yourself of the things you do right."

You control your thoughts. By keeping them positive and focused on all the talents you have, your mind will be energized to keep working. Your brain will tell itself to keep going, even when things get difficult, because it will know you have been successful in the past. By working hard and focusing on your talents, you will be even more successful in the future.

Failure Plus Persistence Equals Success

Tom Hopkins

If you first try something new, most people wouldn't expect you to be perfect at it. In fact, as you learn new things you might be the only person who knows how many times you've tried to be successful. No one will remember your failures because people take note of successes far more often than the number of failures.

Author Tom Hopkins once wrote, "I am not judged by the number of times I fail, but by the number of times I succeed; and the number of times I succeed is in direct proportion to the number of times I fail and keep trying."

Even if you fail several times, success eventually comes from the number of times you try. Each time you learn from your last effort and try again, you refine your skills. For example, you might practice your math skills over and over, until you're ready to be successful on an upcoming test. Your success becomes a great example to others because they'll remember you never gave up.

Choose to Take Action
Nathaniel Howe

The things you choose to do tell a lot about you as a person. For example, doing your best consistently shows you have enormous potential to learn and become great at new things. But if you decide you don't want to do anything, it may mean you are not interested in developing new skills.

Nathaniel Howe once said, "The way to be nothing is to do nothing."

The opposite is true too. The way to become great is to do great things. If you spend time developing your mind by reading and taking on new, increasingly difficult projects, you will respond to wonderful opportunities offered to you in the future. Today, choose to take action and do the things you want to be.

Work Comes Before Success

Vidal Sassoon

The law of cause and effect says that every event has a cause, and one event stimulates a result that would not have occurred without the initial cause. For example, when you plant a seed and water it, you set up the cause that leads to the effect of the growing plant. But in most cases, work must cause success and it is unlikely for anyone to be successful at something without first putting in the effort.

Vidal Sassoon once said, "The only place where success comes before work is in the dictionary."

Even though alphabetically "success" will show up before "work" in the dictionary – that is the only time you'll find success before work. In other words, work is the cause and success is the effect. Today, decide what skills you need to enhance to be successful, and then cause that success to happen by putting in the extra effort and work to make it happen.

Fear of Failure
Babe Ruth

Babe Ruth lived from 1895 to 1948. He became one of the most popular figures in baseball history because he never stopped trying to hit the ball. In 1927, he set a record by hitting sixty home runs in a single season. Previously, he hit at least fifty home runs in four separate seasons and at least forty in each of eleven seasons.

Babe Ruth once said, "Never let the fear of striking out get in your way."

Risk exists in everything you try. But Babe Ruth didn't let the risk of striking out prevent him from trying to hit the baseball. He kept trying and became very successful. Likewise, if you keep trying, you will be successful. Those who worry about making mistakes, however, won't have as much success as those who keep trying no matter what happens. Consistent effort makes the difference between success and failure.

Extremely Inquisitive
Albert Einstein

Albert Einstein is considered one of the greatest scientists to have ever lived. Einstein once said, "I have no particular talent. I am merely extremely inquisitive."

Inquisitiveness leads to unexpected, wonderful new worlds because someone who asks questions will get more information than someone who chooses not to think about new things. Albert Einstein considered his gift to be inquisitiveness. By asking questions and wondering how things work, he achieved great success. He won the Nobel Prize in 1921 and made countless contributions to science.

By being inquisitive you too can bring about new advances in any field you wish to study.

Success Buys a Ticket to the Next Challenge
Henry Kissinger

As each year passes in school, you and your fellow students are expected to master a year's worth of lessons. The challenges naturally become greater as you continue to the following year, moving from elementary levels to secondary levels.

Your progress can be measured through your ability to handle more and more difficult problems. You can't expect your work to become easier, because if it did you wouldn't be challenged at an increasingly higher level.

Henry Kissinger once said, "Each success only buys an admission ticket to a more difficult problem."

So each time you successfully pass a grade level, you can only expect more challenging work in the next. If you do not feel challenged, look for more difficult reading material when you go to the library or the bookstore. Look for new projects that stretch your abilities. Each success enhances your skills and puts you in a position to take on more complex problems.

Luck Comes From Hard Work

Thomas Jefferson

Thomas Jefferson was the third president of the United States. Throughout his career, he did many important things that helped shape the United States. For example, he wrote the Declaration of Independence, served as governor of Virginia, supported the Bill of Rights, became Secretary of State under President Washington, and commissioned Lewis and Clark to lead an expedition across the Louisiana Purchase. Jefferson was also a scientist, inventor, linguist, and architect. He established the University of Virginia and his huge collection of books formed the foundation of the Library of Congress. So how did Jefferson accomplish so many things? Was he just lucky?

Thomas Jefferson once said, "I'm a great believer in luck, and I find the harder I work, the more I have of it."

Maybe he was lucky, but luck comes regularly to those who work hard. People who don't give up become more successful. For example, Thomas Jefferson lost the 1796 election to John Adams. But he served as Adams' vice president, and then ran for president again in 1800. This time, his hard work paid off and he served two terms as America's third president.

Working hard and not giving up will make you continually lucky and successful as you face new challenges.

Look For New Challenges
Pat Riley

Constantly look for new challenges, take on new hobbies, and refine your skills in your favorite sport, because if you are not learning and growing, boredom sets in. Even if you're really good at something, you must continue to improve and expand yourself. It feels great to be a success at something. However, problems arise when people stop challenging themselves after showing they are good at something.

Basketball coach and author Pat Riley wrote, "The temptation to slack off starts when you're feeling good about who you are and what you've achieved. After you have spent yourself emotionally and physically to achieve the great dream, it's so easy to accept the illusion that the struggle has ended."

Pat Riley advises people to constantly look for new challenges. Those who reach great goals may feel like they can stop their learning and training, but anyone who stops will lose their momentum to do their best and may give less of an effort when the next challenge comes their way.

Even if you have achieved great success, look for new challenges today that keep you motivated to achieve greater and greater heights.

Fortune Favors the Bold
Virgil

The great Roman poet Virgil was born in 70 BC. He was a success because he chose to work extremely hard and for long periods of time to do the very best he could. For example, he worked for nearly ten years composing a work called the *Eclogues*. He worked for seven years writing a work called the *Georgics*. Then the last years of his life were devoted to writing his epic poem, *Aeneid*.

Virgil once wrote, "Fortune favors the bold."

He was bold enough to write, reread, revise, and improve his writings. He forced himself to keep working and to challenge himself, even when it was far easier to do something once and stop. That's why we remember him and his writing after thousands of years. So today, be bold enough to revise and re-try your projects. If you force yourself to give extra effort in an area where you are challenged, then you will have the great fortune of success.

A Rough Road Leads to Greatness

Seneca

Seneca was a Roman philosopher, statesman, and playwright who lived from 4 BC to 65 AD. He was also a tutor to the future emperor Nero, and wrote many important philosophical works and plays that influenced writers for centuries to come.

Seneca once wrote, "It is a rough road that leads to the heights of greatness."

The rough road to greatness includes lots of hard work and effort. For example, you might have to practice every day and tryout year after year before you make the cut for the football team. Or you might have to study a particularly difficult subject for an extra hour every day to get a good grade. Those that become successful are the ones who overcome all the challenges along the road with hard work and persistence.

Be a Good Example
Albert Schweitzer

A lbert Schweitzer was a doctor, author, missionary, and musician. He won many awards for his efforts to help people all over the world, including the Nobel Peace Prize in 1952. He used the money he was awarded and money he earned from public speaking to found and expand hospitals in Africa – specifically helping those with leprosy and African sleeping sickness.

Albert Schweitzer once said, "Example is not the main thing in influencing others; it is the only thing."

Albert Schweitzer believed all life should be respected and loved. This is why he spent his time and energy helping people and setting a great example of how one person can make a big difference in the lives of others. Today, think of one way you can help someone, then do it and set an example for your classmates. If everyone used their talents to help others every day, the world would be a better place.

Effort

Nido Qubein

Nido Qubein couldn't speak English when he came to the United States from the Middle East as a teenager. But he worked hard to overcome his language barrier and went on to become president of the National Speakers' Association and the youngest member inducted into the International Speakers' Hall of Fame.

Nido Qubein once said, "If what you're working for really matters, you'll give it all you've got."

Think about the reasons why you do things like schoolwork and studying. If you keep in mind the benefits that will come from your hard work, you'll find the energy to put in even more effort. When your brain hears you really want to learn and improve your skills, it becomes ready to do a better job. But if your brain is given a negative thought about not wanting to learn, it will not work hard to help you. Today, tell yourself you want to do great things and your brain will help you achieve them.

Your Best Is Not Up to Anyone Else

Hakeem Olajuwon

Hakeem Olajuwon played for the NBA for eighteen years, most of them for the Houston Rockets. He was the third of six children born in Nigeria. His family taught him to be honest, work hard, respect others, and to believe in himself.

Hakeem Olajuwon once said, "I've always felt it was not up to anyone else to make me give my best."

No one can do the work for you, and no one can make you want to give your best. If you want to be a better student, athlete, or friend, only you can decide to put in your best effort. Your friends, teachers, and parents can only support your decision. You must find the desire to succeed within yourself. Today, look inside yourself and decide to give your best effort at being a success.

Preparation Is Half the Victory

Miguel de Cervantes

Miguel de Cervantes was born in Spain in 1547. While fighting in a battle he was injured and his left hand was permanently crippled. Despite this setback, his love of writing led him to create Don Quixote, which is often referred to as the first true modern novel. He wrote for decades before achieving this great level of success, and he regularly improved his skills over time.

Cervantes wrote, "To be prepared is half the victory."

Constant training and preparation to improve your skills will pay off when opportunities arise. You never know when your skills will be useful next, but being prepared will help you meet these challenges. New assignments in school are chances for you to prepare, so use what you are learning now to be prepared for challenges in the future.

You Are Happy When You Enjoy What You're Doing

Dr. Mihaly Csikszentmihalyi

Dr. Mihaly Csikszentmihalyi (pronounced "chick sent me high ee" according to the professor) is a professor at the Drucker School of Management at Claremont University who is known for his theories about how people experience a natural state of flow where they are completely involved in what they are doing.

Flow is a feeling of being happy and fulfilled because you enjoy what you are doing. It means you are using your skills to the utmost, and time flies by quickly as you work. How do you get to the point where you feel happy about what you are doing?

Dr. Csikszentmihalyi has said, "...even without success, creative persons find joy in a job well done. Learning for its own sake is rewarding."

People who try their best feel happy about the experience because of their effort. They try something that they feel is worth doing, they learn from it, and their brain releases chemicals that make them feel great. It doesn't matter if the person is completely successful in their attempt or not, because the real reward comes from the effort involved. Today, make sure to focus completely on what you are doing, give your best effort possible, feel time go by quickly, and find the rewards in your great efforts.

Kites Rise Highest Against the Wind

Sir Winston Churchill

Effort is the key to getting the great results you want, and the greater the effort, the greater the success.

Sir Winston Churchill once said, "Kites rise highest against the wind – not with it."

A kite works against the wind to rise higher and higher because the person flying the kite is making a fantastic effort and using the circumstances he or she is given to create a wonderful result. They use the wind to their benefit, rather than go inside and give up for the day.

If you are given a new challenge and you aren't sure if you are ready for it, put in the effort. You can do amazing things if you try your hardest despite the circumstances.

Time

Quevedo

Time is something you can never get back if you waste it. Spending time thinking about the past, rather than tuning in to what is important now, is a mistake. For example, regretting a bad test score won't help you get better marks in the future. And regretting the friends you've lost won't help you make new friends today.

Spanish poet Quevedo once wrote, "He who spends time regretting the past loses the present and risks the future."

When you waste your time worrying about events from your past, you limit your focus on the events that happen today. Then without strong focus, you cannot perform your current assignments and tasks at the highest level of your ability. Your future depends on how wisely you spend your time and how much effort you put in to each assignment.

Education Is Lighting of a Fire

William Butler Yeats

Poet and playwright William Butler Yeats lived from 1865 to 1939. And even though he won the Nobel Prize for literature in 1923, he continued working hard and improving his writing after he received that distinguished award. Some people stop working really hard after they become successful, but Yeats continued giving his all. He viewed learning as incredibly important and only the start of doing great things.

William Butler Yeats once said, "Education is not the filling of a pail, but the lighting of a fire."

When you learn new ideas, fantastic new possibilities open to you. You can do amazing things using what you learn. Knowledge is a person's first step to solve problems and create wonderful ways to benefit society. Today, remember that everything you learn is just a spark, the very beginning, of fantastic possibilities, and you must use your knowledge to achieve great things and make the world a better place.

Thinking and Revising Creates Possibilities

Henry Ford

Even when you finish a project or a story, you can always find ways to improve it. One of the most important habits of good writers is spending time reviewing and revising. The more you think about how you can improve your work, the greater the number of incredible possibilities you will have.

Henry Ford said, "Thinking always of trying to do more brings a state of mind in which nothing seems impossible."

A short story starts with a small idea that can blossom into a wonderful novel when you revise it and add details. The more success you have from editing your writing, the more confidence you will build for projects in the future. Use your creativity to think of new ways to improve your work. If you consistently think of possibilities, you will have a great habit of doing what others find too difficult.

Magic in Boldness
Johann Wolfgang von Goethe

Starting something new requires you to be brave enough to try. At first, you might feel funny about trying something new, especially if others around you are not doing the same thing. For example, if others are not doing kind things, you might feel uncomfortable doing something kind. But you must be bold enough to start doing what you know is right. The same occurs when you have a great dream to do something amazing when you grow up. It may be difficult to work towards that goal, but you can do it by being bold enough to start.

Johann Wolfgang von Goethe once wrote, "Whatever you can do, or dream you can, begin it. Boldness has genius, power, and magic in it."

When you are bold enough to start working on something new, you will find people who are willing to help you. For example, your teachers give you a great start in building the skills you need. Today, think about what your greatest dream is, figure out the skills you need to achieve that dream, and be brave enough to begin working now. Just by getting started, you will be a great success.

Be Successful Despite Your Obstacles
Ralph Smedley

An amazing number of people in the world overcome obstacles regularly. An obstacle is something that stands in the way of success. For some people, obstacles may be difficulty with a particular subject, and for others it may be a physical disability such as blindness or a hearing impairment.

Ralph Smedley said, "The greater the obstacle, the greater the glory in overcoming it."

Whenever something stands in your way and makes your life difficult, realize that the harder you work to overcome it, the greater your success will feel. Use your creativity to find ways to be successful despite your obstacles. By telling yourself you can be a great success, you help your brain find ways to overcome anything.

The Cycle of Work

Seneca

Seneca, a Roman philosopher from the mid-first century AD, wrote, "Even after a bad harvest there must be sowing."

On farms when the harvest season is over, the work of sowing new crops continues. Even after completing the difficult harvest work, farmers know that if they choose to stop working, there will be no results. They must keep going. Likewise, you must keep going when you start an assignment. Don't allow anything to distract you, because if you stop the results will be less than spectacular or there may be no results at all.

The cycle of hard work keeps going. Today, remember that you choose your results by continuing the cycle of work. If you choose to stop, you won't progress. If you choose to give a great effort, you will achieve great results.

Face Challenges
Dan Rather

Dan Rather is a news reporter and author. He investigates and reports on world events, and through his work, he sees how people work through difficulties to solve their problems.

Dan Rather once wrote, "If all difficulties were known at the outset of a long journey, most of us would never start out at all."

Every journey has difficulties, and part of going through school and accomplishing goals in life means facing challenges. Even though most people don't like difficulties, everyone faces them when they try new things. Today, remember that success occurs when you meet new challenges.

Minds Are Stretched By New Ideas

James Lincoln

Did you know that by reading new and challenging materials you build a bigger brain? Researchers can see size differences in certain parts of the brain in people who spend more time reading and learning than among those who don't spend time learning new things.

James Lincoln once said, "A mind stretched by a new idea never returns to its original dimension."

Your brain is like the muscles in your body; it gets stronger and stronger with use. Reading and thinking about new ideas is a way to provide exercise for your brain that cannot be undone. By continuing to learn new things, you strengthen your brain for future success.

Success Is Ninety-Nine Percent Failure

Soichiro Honda

S oichiro Honda founded the Honda Motor Corporation. He believed in trying new ways of doing things until you have the best possible product. But trying out new ideas means there will inevitably be some ideas that don't work.

Honda once said, "Success is ninety-nine percent failure."

Trying new things means you will probably make mistakes. For example, when you begin a complex math problem that you've never seen before, you will probably make some errors. But if you stick with it, you will master the details and be able to solve similar problems in the future. And when you try a new sport, you will probably need to spend time practicing the basic skills before you are really good.

Today, remember that learning from mistakes is not something to fear. When you keep trying, your mistakes lead you to greater success.

Show You Are Committed to Do Your Best
Tiger Woods

When he was a toddler, Tiger Woods followed his father around the course, and he grew up devoted to practicing his skills. He became a golf legend at a young age due to his commitment to practice. But success was not easy as he started participating in competitions. He was typically the youngest player on the course, and for that reason he felt intimidated by the older, bigger players. But he was known for practicing on the driving range after the sun had set and other players went home.

Tiger explained the lessons he learned from the game of golf: "Do your best. Play fairly. Embrace every activity with integrity, honesty, and discipline. Be responsible for your actions. And, above all, have fun."

Through his commitment to practice and constantly refine his skills at age twenty-one he became the youngest golfer ever to be ranked number one. You can achieve any dream you set your mind to just as Tiger did. The key is to do your best and commit to practice.

You Choose Your Future
Carl Bard

You cannot change the past. If a problem existed yesterday, you cannot go back in time to fix what happened. You can only control your actions right now and in the future.

Carl Bard said, "Though no one can go back and make a brand new start, anyone can start from now and make a brand new ending."

Controlling today and the future makes your choices incredibly important. A great amount of effort today will create great results in the future. But poor effort today will create negative future results. Today, make sure your choices reflect the results you would like to have and you will create your own wonderful future.

Fortune Favors the Audacious
Desiderius Erasmus

Desiderius Erasmus is considered to be the greatest European scholar of the 16th century. Born in Holland, Erasmus became a priest in 1492, studied at the University of Paris, and traveled throughout Europe. He wrote many history books and spoke out against practices he felt were wrong. In doing so, he observed the world changing and recognized that people achieved success when they were bold in their actions.

Erasmus wrote, "Fortune favors the audacious."

Audacious means bold or daring. Erasmus felt that if people aren't bold enough to do what is important to them or to speak out against the mistreatment of others, then nothing will ever improve. Those who try new things are the ones who invent solutions to problems. By being daring, bold, and doing what is right, you can help make the world a better place.

Everything Was First a Thought
Kahlil Gibran

Lebanese-American author Kahlil Gibran wrote, "Everything we see today, made by past generations, was before its appearance, a thought in the mind of a man or an impulse in the heart of a woman."

Everything in existence today started with a thought. Inventions, buildings, vehicles, appliances, and everything else around us originated with an idea in someone's mind. Records are broken first by ideas – someone has to think they can set a new record by doing something faster or differently from those who have done it before.

Dreams, ideas, and possibilities exist inside everyone, just waiting to emerge. These ideas are the building blocks of reality. First comes the idea, and then come the actions that bring ideas into reality. Today, use your ideas to do positive things for others, think of ways to help and you can make the world different tomorrow.

Dream Can Come True
Belva Davis

B elva Davis said, "Don't be afraid of the space between your dreams and reality. If you can dream it, you can make it so."

A great example of this comes from two brothers who worked together to make their dream come true. Neither of the two graduated from high school, and they didn't have a lot of money to finance their dream – they built and fixed bicycles for a living. But on a windy December morning in 1903 they became the first to design, build, and fly an engine-powered airplane without crashing.

Wilbur and Orville Wright weren't afraid to try ways to make their dreams come true, and you can do the same. Students all over the world come up with wonderful new inventions every year.

By taking your wonderful ideas, working through them step-by-step, showing persistence, and keeping up the effort, you can make your dreams come true.

Courage Is Resistance to Fear

Seneca

Courage is often associated with heroic acts where people save the lives of others. But courage is also required to do things others don't think you can do. Seneca wrote, "Courage is resistance to fear, mastery of fear, not absence of fear."

College professor Dr. Marigold Linton is an example of someone who showed this type of courage and faced her fear of failure. As an American Indian, Marigold Linton grew up on a reservation where children went to school but rarely went on to college. Since everyone around her said she couldn't do it and she had the enormous pressure of being the first from her reservation to actually attend college, Marigold spent all her time studying and trying her hardest. Even though she studied constantly, she was shocked when her report card showed she earned A's in every class. She kept up her success, earned a doctorate at UCLA, and taught college courses at San Diego State University and the University of Utah.

Marigold would not have been successful without showing she had the courage to do what others told her she could never do. With effort and courage anything is possible.

Do Your Best
Olympic Creed

Winning is not always the ultimate goal, but doing your best whenever you participate in anything is the great challenge.
In fact, Olympic athletes are reminded of this through the Olympic Creed:

"The most important thing in the Olympic Games is not to win but to take part, just as the most important thing in life is not the triumph, but the struggle. The essential thing is not to have conquered but to have fought well."

You can use this creed to guide you throughout the day. For example, even when your team doesn't score the highest in physical education class, the essential part of the game is that you put your best effort forth. Do your best no matter what, as the essential thing is using your skills the best you can.

Dreams Make a Difference Regardless of Age

Makenzie Snyder

You are never too young to help others. For example, Makenzie Snyder was only in second grade when she entered a contest about what she would do to make the world a better place. She began a project that would provide a duffel bag and a stuffed animal for every foster child in the United States.

Makenzie said, "My dream is for all the foster-care kids in the entire United States to receive a duffel bag and a cuddly friend. I know it can be done if everyone helps out. It is a lot of work but I never get tired of it."

Makenzie has been on the cover of the *Washington Post*, on television to talk about her project, and has met with government officials, including former President Bill Clinton. All of these people encouraged her efforts. Her website www.childrentochildren.org has attracted attention from many groups of young people who have helped her meet her goal.

Your goals can be achieved just like Makenzie's. Think about who can help you achieve your goals and ask for their help, because you can make a big difference in the world regardless of your age.

The First Step

Rabona Turner Gordon

R abona Turner Gordon wrote the following poem entitled, "The First Step":

"To take the first step
is a frightening thing.
To face the unknown
The uncertainty it brings.
But like the child
Who is tired of the crawl,
The first step is
The most important of all.
It expands your horizons,
You can see a new light.
The joy of discovery
Is like taking flight.
The first step you take
Will open all doors,
To see yourself as
You've seen you before."

After writing it, she received many letters from people who were reminded by her poem that it is crucial to get started doing something wonderful, no matter how scary the first step might be. This poem can remind you, too, that even as you take the first steps in doing something new, expect to be challenged, like a child who takes his or her first few steps. There may be times when you fall, but if you stay focused on your dream you will be successful. You just need to be brave enough to take the first step.

If You Don't Follow Your Dream, You'll Regret It

Bill Nye, The Science Guy

Do you know who Bill Nye, "The Science Guy," is? His dream was to use his comedic talents to improve people's understanding of science and engineering, and he left a great engineering job to focus on writing and performing. Since that decision, he went on to earn many awards for having an enormous impact on how children view science.

In thinking about his decision to leave his engineering job and follow his dream, Bill Nye once said, "You just reach a point where if you don't do it, you'll regret it."

For him, leaving his job was a big step. But the biggest step in following a dream is often the first. Once you get started pursuing something, you must continue putting forth the effort. You will always experience difficulties along the way, but those are really just tests to check if you are committed to your dream or not. You can be like Bill Nye by doing something that you know you'll enjoy and will make a huge difference in the world.

Get Around the Right People

Brian Tracy

Author Brian Tracy said, "Get around the right people. Associate with positive, goal-oriented people who encourage and inspire you."

In other words, your friends inevitably influence your success. Who are your friends? Do your friends complete their schoolwork successfully, or do they waste their time at school on disruptive activities? Do your friends help you get your work done, or do they distract you when you should be working? If your friends try to distract you from your work, you should take the lead and show them how to be good listeners and follow directions. And if you experience difficulty in your work habits, make friends with those who pay attention.

Today, spend time with people who inspire you to do great things, rather than those who distract you from success.

Helping Others Makes You Happier and Healthier
John D. Rockefeller

John D. Rockefeller, who was one of the wealthiest people in history, started working as a clerk for $3.75 per week. Even when he made a small amount of money, he would give as much as half of his wages to his church every week to help people. He became amazingly wealthy in the years that followed and continued donating money to his church for charity.

When he was fifty-two years old, his doctors told him he had less than a year to live. Upon hearing this, he realized how happy he felt when he gave money to his church and helped others. So he sold half of his stock in the Standard Oil Company and donated the money to charity. Then something amazing happened. The more money he gave away, the better Rockefeller felt. His health improved, he recovered completely, and he lived to age ninety-one in excellent health. By the time he died, he had given away millions of dollars and was extremely happy.

Today, make sure to help someone else, because you become happier when you help others. When you are happy, you become healthier as well because your mind and body know good things are happening.

Try New Things No Matter What Your Age
Albert Schweitzer

If you decide today to be a doctor, sports figure, writer, teacher, plumber, engineer, or some other profession, do you always have to stick to that profession? NO. You can choose to be anything you want at any time in your life. Albert Schweitzer is a great example of this. In the late 1800s, he was the top Bach organist in Europe and only thirty years old. Schweitzer was a musical superstar who drew many people to see him play in all the great capital cities of Europe. But at the height of his musical career, he wanted to make a greater difference with his life.

At that time, at the end of the nineteenth century, news of disease and devastation in Africa filled the newspaper and magazines. So Schweitzer decided to become a medical missionary. He went back to school and devoted eight years of his life to earn a degree in tropical medicine, while he played concerts on the side to raise money. At age thirty-eight he loaded his medical supplies on a ship and sailed to Africa. When he arrived, he set up a tent in a village called Lambarene and worked as a doctor. He stayed in Africa for fifty-three years and became famous for helping people who needed it most. Within ten years of his death, more hospitals were named after him in the world than for any other person.

Schweitzer was a success because he changed careers in his thirties. If you have a lot of things you want to be, don't ever think you have to choose just one career. You can start one and then move to another; you just have to be willing to keep learning, studying, and trying new things.

Response to Pressure
Shane Murphy

Shane Murphy is a famous soccer coach who has played, coached, and written about the sport for most of his life. He said, "If things start going wrong, having a consistent approach prevents panic. (Don't change) the way you do things because of pressure."

When people around you try to do something wrong and want you to do the same thing, don't panic. When others pressure you, you can still control your response and make good choices. For example, some people might tell you that experimenting with drugs will make you feel good, or that vandalizing property and stealing will make you cool, but these people are wrong.

Doing things you know are wrong won't make you feel good about yourself. And you let yourself down when you give in to pressure from others. But you feel good when you do what you know is right. When you face a challenge, such as peer pressure, and succeed, you feel good. Make choices that make you proud of yourself. If you usually do what's right, keep making those good choices and you will set a good example for others.

The Human Spirit Needs to Triumph to Be Happy

Ben Stein

Ben Stein once said, "The human spirit needs to accomplish, to achieve, to triumph to be happy."

The word "triumph" means "great success." But did you notice that the word triumph begins with a variation of the word "try"? So to be triumphant at something, you first have to try. Researchers have learned that students who don't try new things are not as successful in school. These students often tell themselves that they don't want to try and are scared they might fail. Challenging areas often include speaking in front of a large group and trying a new sport. But when you hesitate to try something, think of the great feeling you'll experience after taking on a new challenge. If you never try new things, you will never experience the sense of excitement and adventure that challenges bring.

You can only triumph if you really try your best to accomplish new things. To get the most out of life, people need to accomplish good things and be happy.

Creativity Is Delicate
Alexander Osburn

Have you ever made fun of someone who had an idea or an answer in class that sounded silly or different? Maybe you've had an idea that someone else has made fun of. Sometimes people naturally react to new ideas with teasing, but that doesn't mean that one idea is better than another. Creativity starts with new and different ideas. When you make fun of someone who has an idea, you discourage them from sharing their creative thoughts.

Alexander Osburn said, "Creativity is so delicate a flower that praise tends to make it bloom, while discouragement often nips it in the bud. Any of us will put more and better ideas if our efforts are appreciated."

Creative solutions to problems and issues can make the world a better place for everyone. Today, recognize that creativity needs encouragement and help others be more creative by listening to their ideas.

Rewards Are in Proportion to Service
Earl Nightingale

Earl Nightingale wrote about how people reach their goals. He said, "We will receive not what we idly wish for but what we justly earn. Our rewards will always be in exact proportion to our service."

This means if you really want something, like an "A" on your next test, then you can't just sit around wishing for it. You have to put effort into getting the things you want the most. You can't just wish for good grades and understanding. You earn the things you want the most by trying, listening, and doing good work.

Expect Success
Jim Stovall

Jim Stovall is an author and speaker who started a television network that focuses on making television shows and movies accessible for people with vision problems. Stovall was also a weightlifter who participated in the Olympics. Are you surprised to hear that he is blind?

Jim Stovall shows that nothing is impossible through the great things he does. He once said, "You get what you expect. Expect success."

Everyone has limitations like Stovall. Some of you may face challenges in a particular subject, while others may have learning disabilities or physical disabilities that make school work extremely difficult. But these limitations can be overcome and you can be successful. If you expect to be a success no matter what problems you face, you will get what you expect.

Are You Willing to Do Your Best?
Colin Powell

Freedom means the ability to make choices. You can choose to be your best or your worst, but ultimately the decision is yours. For example, you can choose to help or not to help. You can choose to get in trouble today or to have one of the best days you've ever had.

Secretary of State Colin Powell once said, "Freedom to be your best means nothing unless you're willing to do your best."

You should use your freedom to choose to be the best, most successful person you can be. Today, show you've chosen to be your best by doing your best in every challenge that is set before you.

Truth Never Damages
Mahatma Gandhi

Have you ever been tempted to lie about something that happened to avoid getting into trouble? Lying may seem easier than facing the truth, but one lie often leads to more trouble in the future. If you get in trouble, the best thing you can do is tell the truth about what happened. Don't worry about anyone else getting in trouble. If others lie, they will only have more problems and continue to get in trouble.

Mahatma Gandhi once said, "Truth never damages a cause that is just."

Nothing bad can ever come from telling the truth. Even when people who lie think they will make things better, dishonesty only makes a situation worse. Lies hurt others and lead to more lies. By always telling the truth, you can avoid the additional consequences that come from dishonesty.

A Good Reputation

Miguel de Cervantes

Spanish poet, playwright, and novelist, Miguel de Cervantes, once wrote, "A good name is better than riches."

Having a good name means that people can respect and trust you. Everything you do contributes to what others think of you. Stealing, lying, cheating, and mistreating people create a bad name, while trust is built by making positive choices and going out of your way to help. Be helpful, try hard, tell the truth, and be kind to others. If you do these things, others will think positively of you, and if you make a mistake, say you're sorry.

Building a good reputation is very difficult when you do things that harm others. Because your actions help people decide what they think of you, show that you have good qualities and you will have a good name among others.

ARISTOTLE AND HIS PUPIL, ALEXANDER.

Excellence Is a Habit

Aristotle

The great teacher Aristotle once wrote, "We are what we repeatedly do. Excellence, then, is not an act, but a habit."

For example, if you read all the time, then people will know you as a person who loves books. If you repeatedly practice a particular sport, then people will always associate you with that activity. If you practice something properly over and over, you will become excellent at it.

Your lessons in school are designed to give you the practice you need in a variety of subjects. You can become excellent in all these areas if you spend enough time practicing them. Your habits and effort will reveal what you think is important.

Show your teacher you want to develop the habit of excellence by listening and doing all your work every day.

Great People Make You Feel You Can Become Great
Mark Twain

Do you encourage or discourage your friends when they talk about what they want to be in the future? You should never discourage people who want to do amazing things.

Mark Twain wrote, "Keep away from people who try to belittle your ambitions. Small people always do that, but the really great make you feel that you, too, can become great."

People who make fun of other people's goals don't do great things themselves. In a way, those who tease are jealous of the amazing things that other people accomplish. Other times, they are afraid of those who make great attempts because they are reminded that they lack ambition themselves.

If you spend time focusing on your goals, you will draw other goal-oriented people to you. Spend time around people who make you feel that you can do anything you set your mind to, and you can encourage each other. Goal-oriented people will do great things for others and will inspire you to accomplish great things as well.

Show Enthusiasm

Norman Vincent Peale

Great things happen every day. People try new things. Discoveries are made. Problems are solved. New friendships are formed. Notice when good things happen. Smile when someone gets an answer correct in class. Be proud of students who keep trying when a subject gets difficult, and when you see someone who needs help, be eager to assist.

Norman Vincent Peale once said, "As long as enthusiasm holds out, so will new opportunities."

Every time you're enthusiastic and look for positive things to happen, you will find them. By looking for positives in your classroom and doing your best to help others, you make new opportunities for yourself.

Think Positive
Bob Seger

Do you ever notice how both good things and bad things can happen on the same day? For example, you may wake up with a headache, but participate in a fantastic project a few hours later. Or you may get a bad grade on one assignment, but get an exemplary one on a test.

Songwriter Bob Seger once wrote, "Take a lesson from the trees; watch the way they learn to bend with each breeze."

A breeze may come from one side and then another, just like problems that can come up out of nowhere. The secret is to always do your best regardless of which direction the breeze is blowing, because situations can change in an instant. Just like the tree learns to bend with each breeze, you can be ready for something good to happen after something bad happens.

While you never know what might happen next, if you think positively then you increase your chances of having a great day. Even if things happen that you don't like, do the best you can because a positive attitude helps good things happen to you.

Anger Management
W.H. Auden

What can you do when you're angry? Give yourself a time out. Count to ten. Remind yourself that you have choices. If you are angry and do something mean to someone else, be ready to face the consequences for your bad choices.

Since each person is responsible, remember that you have a tiny space in time when you can think before you act. Stop, think about what you could do, and consider if you will make a good choice or a bad choice.

Author W.H. Auden wrote, "Choice of attention – to pay attention to this and ignore that – is to the inner life what choice of action is to the outer. In both cases, a man is responsible for his choice and must accept the consequences, whatever they may be."

What are some of the positive outcomes of taking a time out to think? The positive outcomes include knowing you can make good things happen for yourself and others, knowing you can be a good example, and knowing that your friends will want to be with you because you're making positive choices.

So the next time you feel like you're getting angry, take a time out to think about the consequences of your actions and then make the responsible choice.

Friends
William Rostler

William Rostler once wrote, "How rare and wonderful is that flash of a moment when we realize we have discovered a friend."

It feels great to find a friend because a friend is someone to share your experiences with. You can share your thoughts and feelings with your friends and friends take care of each other.

How do you make and keep friends? One way is to be helpful and supportive. This means you need to understand what someone else wants to do or thinks is important. If you only think of yourself, you won't make and keep friends. If you get upset easily, other people will know you aren't someone who will help solve a problem. So to experience the wonderful moment that comes from finding a friend, be a problem solver and work to help other people. If you do, you'll have many friends.

Trustworthiness

Kingman Brewster

If you are trustworthy, then people know that you will do what you say you will do. You are dependable and you don't tell lies. If you are asked to do something and say you'll do it, the other person knows you will try your best to get it done.

Educator and President of Yale University, Kingman Brewster, once said, "There is no greater challenge than to have someone relying upon you; no greater satisfaction than to vindicate his expectation."

When you meet the expectations of others who trust you, you take on a responsibility to them. You will feel great satisfaction in knowing that they feel they can rely on you. Once you say you will do something, they know that you absolutely will do it. But if that trust is violated because you let the person down, it is difficult to rebuild it.

When you are continually trustworthy, then you will be given increasingly greater responsibilities. The more challenges you meet, the more confidence you will develop. Work on being trustworthy every day and you will never let people down.

Respect

Katy Fischer

Being respectful has to do with how you look at things. You can divide the word "respect" into two little words: "re" means "again" and "spect" has to do with how you look at things, which is why you can call glasses "spectacles" and you can say something amazing to look at is "spectacular." So respect can mean to look at something again in a special way.

Katy Fischer said, "The qualities that make each of us different make each of us special."

Show respect for your friends and family by looking at them in a special way. While they are different from you, they are people who care about you and want you to succeed.

If you respect others, then they will look at you as a special person.

Be a Good Example
Martin Luther King, Jr.

When you do good things you make the world a better place because other people watch and learn from what you do. It's a lot like a honeybee working to obtain nectar to make honey. While flying around to find nectar, the pollen that the bee collects on his wings falls off and helps other plants in the area. This is called cross-pollination. While the honeybee wants to make honey, it also makes the world beautiful by helping create a bountiful garden. Does the bee really know that the pollen falling from his wings improves the beauty around it? Probably not, but it still has a positive effect on the environment.

By doing good things for others, you are like the honeybee that makes the world beautiful. When you are walking to class, working on assignments, and doing good things at school, you improve the entire environment.

Martin Luther King Jr. once said, "The time is always right to do what is right."

Others notice the good things you do and are inspired to follow your good example. You probably won't even see anyone noticing you, but your good choices help make the entire school better.

Teamwork
Patanjali

Do you enjoy watching football? Have you ever noticed that all the players on the team work together towards the same goal? Either they want to advance the ball down the field to score, or they work together to keep the other team from advancing the ball. They all help one another and know each member of the team is important.

Patanjali, an author from India, once said, "When a gifted team dedicates itself to unselfish trust and combines instinct with boldness and effort, it is ready to climb."

Even if a team is losing, they still stick together with unselfish trust. And even if one member of the team drops the ball or makes a mistake, they still work together to win the game. The team who works together, where everyone tries their hardest, is usually the team that wins.

Your class is like a team. Remember that you need to work together with your classmates all year long to make your team great. Today, be a good example and encourage others on your team to do the best they can.

Confidence
Franklin D. Roosevelt

How can you feel confident about the things you do? Franklin D. Roosevelt, the thirty-second president of the United States said, "Confidence...thrives only on honesty, on honor, on the sacredness of obligations, on faithful protection and on unselfish performance. Without them, it cannot live."

He meant that if you are dishonest and do not make sure to do the best you can, you will not be confident in your ability to succeed. The dictionary defines confidence as faith or belief that one will act in a right, proper, or effective way. Today, make sure to do things in the proper way by being honest and trying your best in all you do. If you try your best every day, your confidence will build.

You're Original Because of Your Mind
Earl Nightingale

You're an original. There's no one exactly like you. Why are people different from one another? Some people might say people are different because everyone looks different from others. But identical twins look exactly alike. So what really makes people different from one another?

The dictionary defines someone who is original as, "A person of fresh initiative or inventive capacity."

Author Earl Nightingale once wrote, "Your world is a living expression of how you are using and have used your mind."

So people are really different because of what they think and what they do. The choices each person makes shows what he or she thinks is important. With your choices you can be original and show the world the many ways you are different.

Holidays

Labor Day

Samuel Gompers

L abor Day is the first Monday in September. This special day comes from the labor movement and is dedicated to the achievements of workers in the United States. Labor Day is an annual national tribute to the hard work Americans do to contribute to the strength, prosperity, and well-being of the country.

Samuel Gompers founded and served for a long time as the president of the American Federation of Labor. He said, "Labor Day differs in every essential way from the other holidays of the year in any country. All other holidays are in a more or less degree connected with conflicts... Labor Day...is devoted to no man, living or dead, to no sect, race, or nation."

So this Labor Day, take time to acknowledge the people from the past and present who work hard to be successful in their jobs..

September 11

S pecial days are on the calendar to help us remember important things. September 11th is one of these important days in our country's history where people remember the things that happened that day. These things may make people feel sad, frightened, or angry. The time we spend reflecting is not to make anyone feel badly. Instead, that time can be used to remind us of the positive actions of brave people who wanted to help others.

When thinking about the firefighters, paramedics, police officers, people who were trained in medicine, and those who helped strangers, remember that these people helped because it was the right thing to do. After that day, we saw selflessness in the cards, flowers, and supplies that were sent to comfort others.

While thinking about the events of September 11th may make you feel sad, make sure to remember the way people helped one another. Today, take the time to help someone else, even if the person is a stranger.

Veterans Day

Veterans Day was originally known as Armistice Day to honor the veterans of World War I and was identified as a holiday in 1938. In 1954, after World War II had required the greatest mobilization of soldiers, sailors, marines, and airmen in the Nation's history, the government recognized that all veterans of all wars should be honored by changing Armistice Day to Veterans Day.

So as we recognize Veteran's Day this year, keep in mind that this day is to honor America's veterans for their patriotism, love of country, and willingness to serve and sacrifice for the common good.

Thanksgiving
Anthony Robbins

Author Anthony Robbins said Thanksgiving is about, "giving good thanks, not eating turkey."

Anthony Robbins' family was so poor growing up that on Thanksgiving a stranger came to his house with a huge box of food, a giant turkey, and cooking pans for his family. He was so thankful for the generosity showed to his family when they were in need that he started his own tradition when he was older. He really wanted to give thanks for what he had by sharing food with those who need it most on Thanksgiving. Each Thanksgiving Anthony Robbins loads up a van with food and goes to the neediest people in the poorest areas as his special way of giving thanks.

What is your special way of showing others you are thankful on Thanksgiving? This Thanksgiving do nice things for others and make sure you share what you are thankful for with the people you love.

Winter Break

May Sarton

Poet May Sarton wrote, "A holiday gives one a chance to look backward and forward, to reset oneself by an inner compass."

She meant that each person has a chance to reset themselves, deciding what has gone well this year and choosing what to focus on for improvement in the year to come. During the break, think of three ways you can improve. For example, can you read more at home? Can you keep a journal to practice writing every day? Can you help your family keep the house clean? Do you need to improve in math or science? Can you take the time to read books about people who are doing what you would like to do someday?

Think of three ways you can improve over the break and get started. If you keep those things in mind every day, you'll be amazed at how much you can improve yourself within one year. Then, you can reset yourself again with new goals next year.

President's Day
Abraham Lincoln

How many elections did Abraham Lincoln lose before he became the sixteenth president of the United States? He lost six times in state and national elections. But even though he lost many times, he never gave up.

As President's Day approaches, remember that all the presidents of the United States risked losing elections to become president. If they were too afraid to lose, they would never have run for office. On this holiday take a moment to remember that each president had to keep trying until they became successful.

You can do the same. If you have an assignment that is difficult today, don't give up. Keep trying until you succeed.

Memorial Day

Did you know that Memorial Day was originally called Decoration Day? When the day was first observed on May 30, 1868, it was a time set aside to decorate the graves of those who passed away during the Civil War. Now, this is a day of remembrance for those who died in service to our nation.

Memorial Day is celebrated at Arlington National Cemetery with a special ceremony in which a small American flag is placed on each grave, and either the president or vice-president gives a speech honoring the contributions of those who have passed away. Then they lay a wreath on the Tomb of the Unknown Soldier.

On this Memorial Day, take a moment to remember those who served our country and passed away.

Index

Index

Index

Index

Book Order Form

Fax orders: 661-255-3677. Send this form.

Telephone orders: Call 818-822-7071. Have your credit card ready.

Secure Online Ordering: www.fiszerconcepts.com

Postal Orders: Fiszer Concepts, LLC, 26873 Sierra Highway, Santa Clarita, CA 91321, USA.

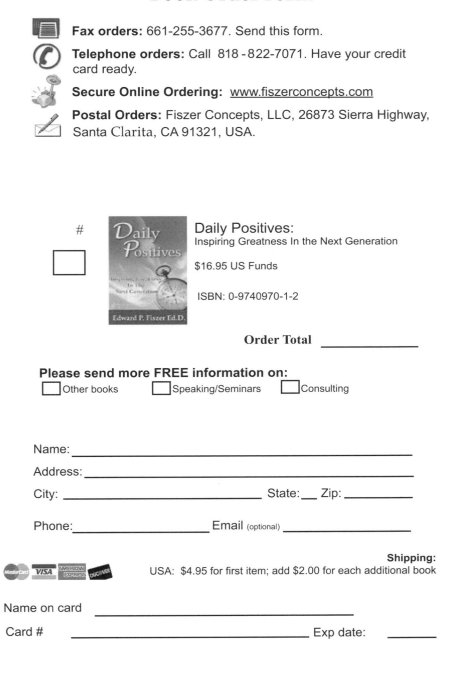

\#

Daily Positives:
Inspiring Greatness In the Next Generation

$16.95 US Funds

ISBN: 0-9740970-1-2

Order Total _____

Please send more FREE information on:

☐ Other books   ☐ Speaking/Seminars   ☐ Consulting

Name: _____

Address: _____

City: _____ State: ___ Zip: _____

Phone: _____ Email (optional) _____

Shipping:
USA: $4.95 for first item; add $2.00 for each additional book

Name on card _____

Card # _____ Exp date: _____